Competitiveness of South Asia's Container Ports

**DIRECTIONS IN DEVELOPMENT**
Infrastructure

# Competitiveness of South Asia's Container Ports

*A Comprehensive Assessment of Performance, Drivers, and Costs*

Matías Herrera Dappe and Ancor Suárez-Alemán

**WORLD BANK GROUP**

# Contents

## Boxes

## Figures

**Map**

**Tables**

# Foreword

South Asia ranks far behind East Asia and middle-income countries in logistics performance as tracked by the 2014 *Logistics Performance Index*, while according to *Doing Business*, the cost of exporting or importing a container in South Asia is more than twice the cost in East Asia.

These figures matter for South Asia, a region where 75 percent of the international trade takes place by sea. As China is shifting out of labor-intensive sectors such as apparel, South Asia has the potential to capture a growing share of the global market. This may in turn attract more foreign direct investment, increase trade and diversify exports, and create new jobs for South Asia's growing labor force. But tapping into these opportunities will require removing bottlenecks in transport logistics, and ports in particular.

The World Bank is helping governments in the region improve transport logistics and infrastructure through: capacity building programs for transport agencies; roads, railways, and waterway performance enhancements; and the creation of seamless networks connecting production and consumption centers. Improving the performance of ports and removing bottlenecks hindering the flow of imports and export is key to that effort; it is also critical for the integration of isolated regions and landlocked countries in the global economy.

Earlier analytical work on port performance in South Asia has been confined mainly to case studies, with a limited set of ports, short timeframes, and narrow focus on performance and its drivers. The analysis in this report, the first of its kind covering South Asia, makes use of a novel and comprehensive dataset to thoroughly assess the performance of the 14 largest container ports in the region, which represent 98 percent of container traffic.

The report shows that improving logistics performance in the region through measures that increase the efficiency of container ports would boost trade to and from South Asia and would therefore support South Asia on its path to become a dynamic middle-income region, building on an increasingly dynamic private sector using the regional ports as nodes for regional and global commerce.

The reform agenda identifies issues of port management structure and ownership models, port infrastructure improvements, policy and regulatory frameworks for transport logistics, general sector governance, as well as port-hinterland connectivity. The enabling environment in the South Asian port sector has been evolving over the last two decades. Improvements that can be further built on include removal of market access restrictions, higher efficiency of border management, better use of information and communication technologies (ICT), and business environment reforms.

Analysis presented in this report should help policy makers in South Asia in creating an environment conducive to high port performance, allowing deeper integration into global markets for higher prosperity in South Asia.

Pierre Guislain
*Senior Director*
*Transport and ICT Global Practice*
*The World Bank*

# Acknowledgments

This report was prepared by a team led by Matías Herrera Dappe (Senior Economist, Transport and ICT Global Practice). The core team included Ancor Suárez-Alemán and Fernanda Ruiz Nuñez. The extended team included Paul Amos, María Cabrera Escalante, Charl Jooste, Rashi Grover Kashyap, Aman Khanna, Edward T. Liang, Sebastian López-Azumendi, Gouthami Padam, and Jamie Andrew Simpson. Administrative support was provided by Comfort Onyeje Olatunji. Barbara Karni and Datapage provided editorial and manuscript preparation support.

The team thanks the following colleagues for their helpful contributions, comments, and suggestions: Luis Alberto Andrés, Bernard Aritua, Arnab Bandyopadhyay, Reynaldo Bench, Benedictus Eijbergen, Esteban Ferro, Diep Nguyen-Van Houtte; Amali Rajapaksa, Tomás Serebrisky (Inter-American Development Bank), Bruce Owen Thomson, Lourdes Trujillo (University of Las Palmas de Gran Canaria), John Wilson (Center for Global Enterprise), and Hasan Afzal Zaidi.

The team is grateful to Martin Rama, the South Asia Regional Chief Economist, and Karla González Carvajal, the South Asia Transport and ICT Practice Manager, for their support and guidance. Peer reviewers Jean François Arvis, Dan Biller, and Gylfi Palsson provided insightful and constructive comments. Financial support from the Australian government is gratefully acknowledged.

# About the Authors

**Matías Herrera Dappe** is a senior economist in the Transport and ICT Global Practice of the World Bank. He has worked in the field of infrastructure and economic policy for more than 10 years, focusing on the economics of infrastructure investment, private sector participation in infrastructure, performance benchmarking, competition, regulation, and auctions. Before joining the World Bank, he worked with private firms and think tanks and as an independent consultant, advising governments and private firms in Latin America, North America, and Europe. He has published extensively on the topics mentioned. He holds a PhD in economics from the University of Maryland, College Park.

**Ancor Suárez-Alemán** is an economist whose research focuses on infrastructure, transport policy, port economics, efficiency, competition, and regulation. He has consulted on infrastructure projects for the Spanish government, the European Union, the World Bank, and the Inter-American Development Bank. His research has been published in a number of peer-reviewed journals. He holds a PhD in economics from the University of Las Palmas de Gran Canaria in Spain.

# Executive Summary

South Asia's trade almost doubled in the past decade, with trade as a percentage of GDP increasing by 18 percentage points between 2000 and 2014. Since 2000 the region has also enjoyed the second-highest economic growth in the world (after East Asia), growing at an average annual rate of 6.8 percent.

Despite this progress, trade accounted for a smaller share of GDP in South Asia (47 percent) than in East Asia (55 percent) in 2014, and South Asia's economic competitiveness continued to lag behind that of other regions. Global indicators, such as the *Global Competitiveness Report*, point to shortcomings in the institutional, business, and investment environments and highlight concerns that the region may not have the infrastructure needed to compete more successfully in the global economy. In all countries in the region except Sri Lanka, such indicators rank inadequate infrastructure among the most problematic factors for doing business.

**Weak transport and logistics services, including slow expansion of port capacity, contribute to South Asia's lack of competitiveness.**

On the 2014 Logistics Performance Index, South Asia trails both East Asia and middle-income countries in logistics performance, particularly in the infrastructure component. According to the *Doing Business* report, the average cost of exporting or importing a container in the region as a whole is more than twice the cost in East Asia.

Better port logistics in South Asia could help increase trade, diversify exports, attract more foreign direct investment (FDI), and spur economic growth. Companies that trade internationally depend crucially on supply and export chains that run through ports. About 75 percent of South Asia's trade by value is transported by sea, and even some intraregional trade goes by sea. How ports perform affects the time, cost, and efficiency of trade, which partly determine the level of global competitiveness and the volume of trade. The effects of port performance extend to the competitiveness of industries in hinterlands, including in the region's landlocked nations.

As a result of the impressive growth in trade in South Asia since 2000, container traffic in the region increased by a factor of more than four. Capacity also increased, but it grew much more slowly than cargo growth. Indeed, only the economic slowdown wrought by the 2008 global financial crisis eased pressures on capacity.

As container traffic keeps growing and physical expansion is constrained by the limited supply of available land in most ports, increasing the productivity of port facilities becomes critical. How to do so to accommodate a large portion of the anticipated increase in container traffic presents an important challenge to port operators and port authorities.

**Container port performance in South Asia is better than it was—but there is still much room for improvement, particularly at lagging ports.**

Tariffs and terminal handling charges at most large South Asian container ports are lower than those at ports such as Dubai, Salalah, and Singapore. But the indirect costs associated with delays, loss of markets and customer confidence, and opportunities forgone to inefficient service play a more significant role in shippers' port choices.

As a consequence of the growth in traffic, congestion at container ports across South Asia increased between 2000 and 2012. Ports have offset longer waiting times by improving the efficiency of their operations at the berthing stage. More efficient use of port facilities, together with improvements in the scale of operations, were the main drivers of increases in total factor productivity (TFP) in South Asia. These increases helped South Asia catch up with East Asia in terms of efficiency in the use of facilities. On average, South Asian container ports experienced the largest improvement in TFP among ports in the Indian and Western Pacific Oceans (80 percent versus 55 percent for East Asia) between 2000 and 2010.

South Asia still has significant potential to improve overall efficiency in the container port sector through scale expansion, as demonstrated by the fact that 62 percent of its container ports showed increasing returns to scale between 2008 and 2010. In 2010, the region's ports could have handled twice the throughput they did with existing facilities.

Port performance varies across South Asia. Some ports, such as Colombo, Jawaharlal Nehru Port, Mundra, and Qasim, improved the use of their facilities between 2000 and 2010. Others, such as Mumbai and Tuticorin, fell further behind. Colombo—which also improved its operational performance during this period by almost halving the share of idle time at berth—ranked as one of the top South Asian ports in 2010 in terms of operational and economic performance. Chittagong and Kolkata, which performed well in terms of the use of their facilities in 2010, ranked poorly on operational performance, with the longest vessel turnaround times in the region.

**Private sector participation, good governance, and strong competition are key drivers of performance.**

Private sector participation, port governance, and competitive forces all tend to be related to higher levels of operational and economic performance of ports. Many other factors are also at play, including trade flows, distance to markets, and custom regulations, but these factors are not directly controllable by port authorities or shipping ministries. In contrast, private participation and governance structures are national or local policy choices. The contestability of port services is clearly influenced by the proximity to other ports, but policy choices can either support or inhibit both interport and intraport competition.

The evidence on South Asia supports global findings that ports at which the private sector provides services to shipping companies (so-called landlord ports) attain higher levels of operational performance and economic efficiency than ports run based on other models. Beginning in the late 1990s/early 2000s, India, Pakistan, and Sri Lanka reformed their port sectors, introducing private sector participation. Bangladesh is the only country on the Indian subcontinent that has not adopted the landlord model.

Large and medium-size landlord ports performed better than other types of port on average. Application of the landlord model has varied, however, as have performance and investment experiences. Understanding the particular aspects behind implementation of the landlord model at each port is key to designing effective concrete actions.

Ports that have better-governed port authorities with more transparent appointment processes and independent members also perform better. The boards of the best-performing South Asian ports exhibit high levels of professionalization, and the ports they serve have higher levels of private sector investment. Even at landlord ports, port authorities' boards generally have responsibility (either directly or through service contracts) for ancillary services, such as tugging, pilotage, facilities for freight forwarders and customs inspections, and road and rail connectivity to the port. When performed well, all of these roles facilitate better operational performance. Effective boards seem to understand the interlinked nature of the public and private contributions to ensuring timely and efficient movement of cargo through ports.

A more competitive environment is also associated with better performance of container ports in South Asia. Competition is stimulated at the initial concession stage—through open bidding—and through port policy objectives that introduce new operators as port expansion proceeds. In contested hinterlands, such as northwest India, interport competition is a powerful force for improving port performance and investment.

In South Asia, ports that operated in more competitive environments during 2000–10 were, on average, more efficient in the use of their facilities. Ships at ports in more competitive environments also spent less time on average at port.

These results are in line with the intuition that ports operating in more competitive environments need to operate at higher levels of economic and operational performance to attract traffic.

**A three-pronged approach that strengthens private sector participation, governance, and competition promises to yield the greatest improvement in South Asia's container ports.**

Ports in South Asia have modernized, but more needs to be done to meet the growth and competitiveness challenge. Experience from across the globe, including the South Asian experience discussed in this report, indicates that a comprehensive approach that tackles several interrelated angles yields greater benefits than isolated improvements. A promising three-pronged approach for improving performance in the region would (a) encourage private sector participation through a well-developed enabling environment, including further adoption of the landlord port model; (b) strengthen governance of port authorities' boards; and (c) promote competition between and within ports, in part through transparent and competitive concession bidding.

Strong governance and capacity of port authorities are requisites for the successful implementation of the landlord port model. Moving from a public sector monopoly to an unregulated private sector monopoly will not bring efficiency gains. Increases in private sector participation should go hand in hand with increased competition for the market and in the market. Where competition in the market is limited because of large economies of scale relative to the size of the market, efficiency gains should come through adequate regulation.

**Improving performance of existing container ports would increase South Asia's global competitiveness.**

Governments interested in increasing the competitiveness of their exports need to improve the performance of their transport networks in order to reduce overall trade and transport costs, including the indirect costs caused by delays and unreliability. Countries with more efficient port sectors incur lower maritime transport costs in their exports. A 0.1 unit increase in the average efficiency score of a country's port sector (on a scale on which 0 is most inefficient and 1 is most efficient) would reduce the maritime transport cost of its exports by 2.3 percent, leading to a 1.8 percent increase in exports.

If the port sectors of Bangladesh, India, and Pakistan had been as efficient as the port sector of Sri Lanka during 2000–07, their average maritime transport costs to the United States would have been 0.6–8.8 percent lower. As a consequence, the average value of exports by Bangladesh, India, and Pakistan to the United States would have been 0.5–7.0 percent higher. The potential gains associated with improving port performance are substantial.

# Abbreviations

| | |
|---|---|
| BGI | board governance index |
| BOT | build-operate-transfer |
| CPA | Chittagong Port Authority |
| DEA | data envelopment analysis |
| GDP | gross domestic product |
| i.i.d. | independent and identically distributed |
| IT | idle time at berth |
| JNPT | Jawaharlal Nehru Port |
| NIT | nonidle time at berth |
| OECD | Organisation for Economic Co-operation and Development |
| PPI | Private Participation in Infrastructure |
| PPIAF | Public-Private Infrastructure Advisory Facility |
| PPP | public-private partnership |
| SAGT | South Asia Gateway Terminal |
| SAR | special administrative region |
| SLPA | Sri Lanka Ports Authority |
| TAMP | Tariff Authority for Major Ports |
| TAT | turnaround time |
| TEU | 20-foot equivalent unit |
| TFP | total factor productivity |
| WT | waiting time |

*All dollar amounts are U.S. dollars unless otherwise indicated.*

# Introduction

## A Comprehensive Assessment of South Asia's Container Ports

Trade is critical to economic growth—and ports are critical to trade. Indeed, ports handle about 80 percent of global trade by volume and more than 70 percent by value. In a globalized world in which technology and know-how can be easily acquired and the constant search for the most efficient supply chain drives international container flows, the performance of a region's ports relative to that of competing ports is a crucial determinant of growth.

Transport is a key bottleneck to the competitiveness of South Asia. Global indicators, such as the *Global Competitiveness Report*, point to shortcomings in the institutional, business, and investment environments in South Asia and highlight concerns that the region may not have the infrastructure needed to compete more successfully in the global economy. In all countries in the region except Sri Lanka, such indicators rank inadequate infrastructure among the most problematic factors for doing business. On the 2014 Logistics Performance Index, South Asia trails both East Asia and middle-income countries in logistics performance, particularly in the infrastructure component.

This report is a comprehensive assessment of the performance of container ports in South Asia. It shows that improving the performance of South Asian container ports and reducing the cost of moving cargo into and out of the region could have a dramatic effect on exports. Crafting and implementing improvements requires understanding how ports function and identifying the main bottlenecks. Benchmarking the ports in each of South Asia's largest coastal countries is essential to identifying best practices and shortcomings—and learning from both.

During the 1990s, most South Asian coastal countries implemented reforms in the port sector to increase capacity and performance. Although some reforms achieved these objectives, more needs to be done to meet the growth and competitiveness challenge. This report sheds light on the differences in container port performance and capacity increases across South Asia, identifies the role of the enabling environment, and outlines a path to improved performance.

## Analytical Framework

The report examines the performance of the 14 largest container ports in the region, which represent 98 percent of container traffic in the region, based on two sets of criteria: operational performance and economic performance. The analysis is based on an original and comprehensive dataset of performance indicators from a variety of sources (see table C.1 for a list of sources). To measure operational performance, the report benchmarks total time at port, waiting time at port, and idle time as a share of total time at berth. To measure economic performance, it benchmarks productivity and efficiency using two useful techniques: Malmquist total factor productivity decomposition and data envelopment analysis.

The report also identifies the key drivers of port performance and examines how differences in performance across ports are related to those drivers. This analysis is based on an original dataset on private sector participation, governance, and competition in South Asia's container port sector (see table C.1 for a list of sources). To highlight the potential gains from improving performance of container ports, the report uses econometric techniques to isolate the impact of efficiency improvements on maritime transport costs and trade. Figure I.1 depicts the framework of the analysis in the report.

**Figure I.1  Analytical Framework**

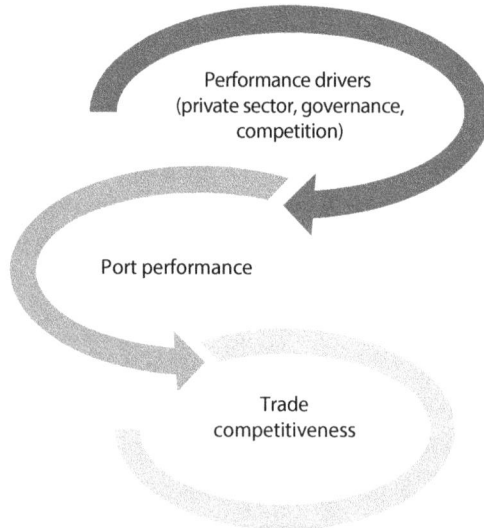

The report answers 10 specific questions:

1. Have South Asian ports become more productive?
2. How do the region's ports perform compare with ports in other regions?
3. Are there productivity differences within the region?
4. What are the sources of productivity changes at South Asian ports?
5. How could ports improve their performance?
6. Have new investments improved performance?

7. Does private sector participation improve port performance?
8. Do port governance characteristics affect port performance?
9. Does port competition contribute to better port performance?
10. How do increases in port efficiency affect transport costs and trade?

## Organization of the Report

This report is organized as follows. Chapter 1 provides an overview of the container port sector in South Asia. It discusses the structure of the sector, the institutional and policy frameworks, investment patterns at the country and regional levels, and port tariffs. Chapter 2 presents a comprehensive assessment of the operational and economic performance of South Asian container ports since 2000 by benchmarking South Asian ports against one another and against other ports in the Indian and Western Pacific Oceans. Chapter 3 examines the most important factors over which port authorities and shipping ministries have control: private sector participation, port governance, and port competition. Chapter 4 estimates the gains from improved port performance.

# CHAPTER 1

# South Asia's Container Port Sector

## Introduction

South Asia is a minor player in global container port traffic. Its importance is growing, however, with its market share rising from 2.1 percent in 2000 to 2.9 percent in 2013.

India is by far the largest container market in the region, moving about 10 million 20-foot equivalent units (TEUs) in throughput in 2013 (figure 1.1).[1] Sri Lanka, whose market is dominated by transshipment, is the next largest player in the region, with throughput of more than 4 million TEUs. Pakistan (2.6 million TEUs) and Bangladesh (1.6 million TEUs) handle smaller volumes of cargo. Maldives handled less than 100,000 TEUs in 2013 (World Development Indicators Database).

The South Asian container traffic grew steadily between 2000 and 2013, increasing by a factor of more than four (figure 1.2). Pakistan's container throughput grew fastest, increasing at a compound annual growth rate of 15 percent. Annual volumes rose 12 percent in India, 10 percent in Bangladesh, 9 percent in Maldives, and 7 percent in Sri Lanka over this period.

The drivers of container throughput in South Asia vary across countries. In Bangladesh export growth led largely by U.S. and European demand for ready-made garments has resulted in throughput growth via the Port of Chittagong and to some extent the Port of Mongla. In India growing exports and increased domestic demand coupled with the increasing involvement of the private sector in port operations has led to increased throughput. Exports of textiles are major drivers of increases in throughput in Pakistan, through the Port of Karachi and Port Qasim. In Sri Lanka productivity improvements caused in part by private sector involvement at the Port of Colombo have allowed it to capture growing volumes of transshipment traffic.

This chapter provides an overview of the container port sector in South Asia. The first section describes the structure of the sector. The second section describes the institutional and policy frameworks. The third section examines investment patterns at the country and regional levels, benchmarking South Asia against other regions. The fourth section looks at port tariffs. The last section provides some concluding remarks.

**Figure 1.1  Distribution of Container Throughput in South Asia, 2013**
*percent*

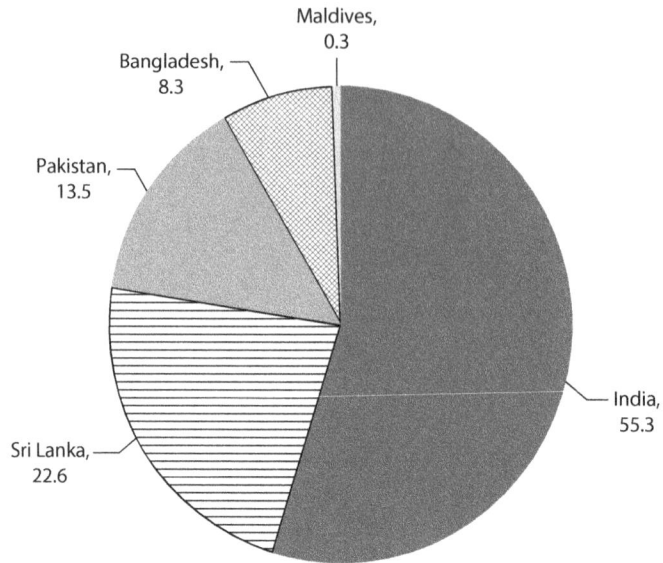

*Sources:* Maldives Port Authority for Maldives; World Development Indicators database for all other countries.
*Note:* Figures are shares of TEUs.

**Figure 1.2  Annual Volume of Container Port Traffic in South Asia, by Country, 2000–13**

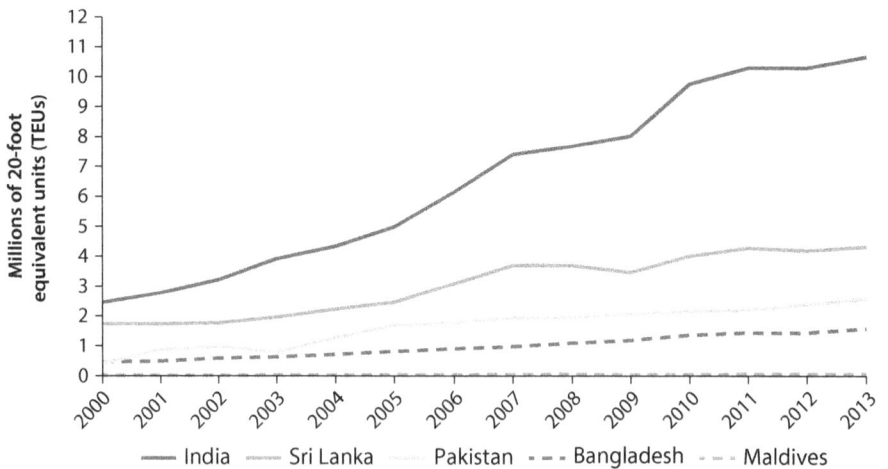

*Sources:* Maldives Port Authority for Maldives; World Development Indicators database for all other countries.

## Structure of the Sector

There are more than 200 ports in South Asia, concentrated largely in India, but only about 20 of them handle more than 9,000 TEUs of containerized cargo annually (map 1.1). All South Asian container ports except for the Port of Colombo handle mostly cargo coming from or going to their hinterland.

Competitiveness of South Asia's Container Ports  •  http://dx.doi.org/10.1596/978-1-4648-0892-0

**Map 1.1  Container Ports in South Asia**

IBRD 41684

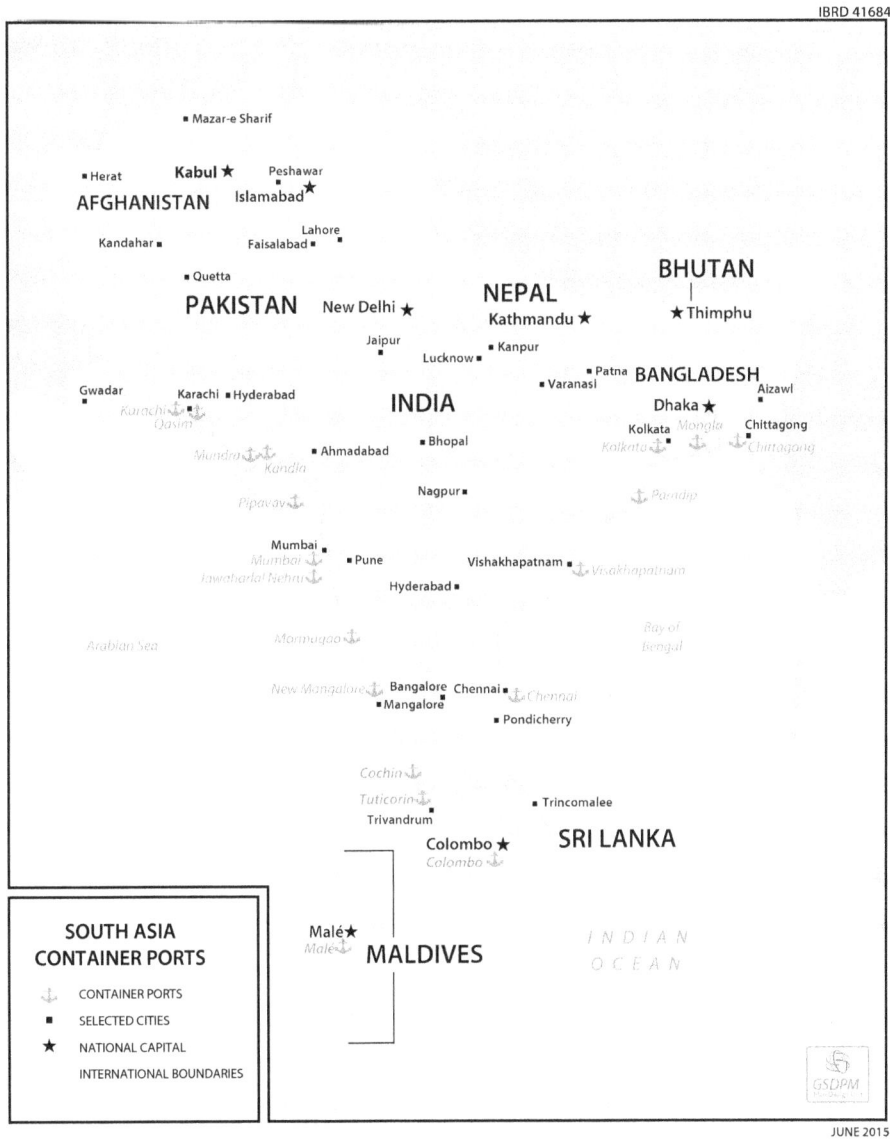

JUNE 2015

## Bangladesh

Bangladesh has just two international ports, Chittagong and Mongla. Mongla's role is limited, as it has a water depth of only 7 meters. In 2013 it handled just 8 percent of container and 10 percent of bulk and break-bulk cargo.

Chittagong is the deepest port in Bangladesh, but at 9.1 meters it is much shallower than its competitors (Colombo, for example, has a depth of 18 meters at its newest terminals, Karachi will have a depth of 16–18 meters at its newest terminal, and the Jawaharlal Nehru Port [JNPT] will be 16 meters deep). As a result,

Bangladesh's exports have to be carried in feeders to the region's hub ports of Colombo, Singapore, and Tanjung Pelepas to link up with deep-sea services. In contrast, the exports of India, Pakistan, and Sri Lanka, all of which have deep water, can use direct services to their main markets. The need to build a deep-water port to improve maritime trade services is a point of debate in Bangladesh.[2]

## India

India has about 200 ports along its 7,500-kilometer long coastline. Thirteen of them handled container throughput levels of 9,000 to more than 4 million TEUs in 2013. About three-quarters of container traffic is handled at ports along India's west coast, particularly in the northwest. The two largest container ports in India—JNPT and Mundra—are on the west coast. The country's third-largest port, Chennai, is located on the east coast (see map 1.1). In 2013 these three ports had throughput of 4.2 million, 2.4 million, and 1.5 million TEUs, respectively (figure 1.3). Pipavav, Tuticorin, and Kolkata lead the second tier of ports (ports with container throughputs of less than 700,000 TEUs).

The three largest container ports have been investing in new terminals with deeper berth depths. The newest container terminal at Chennai

**Figure 1.3  Distribution of Container Throughput in India, 2013**
*percent*

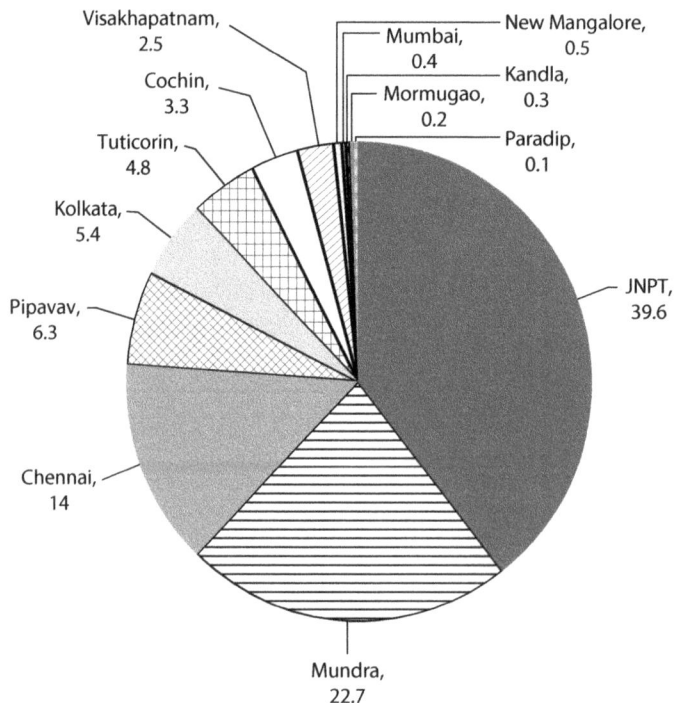

*Source:* Ministry of Road Transport and Highways of India 2014.
*Note:* Figures are shares of TEUs.

(Chennai Container Terminal, which became operational in 2009) has a berth depth of 15.5 meters. The terminals being developed at JNPT and Mundra will have berth depths of 16.5 meters.

### Maldives

Maldives has only one major port, the Malé Commercial Port. Located in the commercial center of the islands, it handles all international cargo except dry bulks, liquefied petroleum, and gases. The majority of cargo is containerized. About 40 percent is distributed from Malé to the outer Maldives islands. The port has a draft of 10.5 meters and can handle vessels up to about 2,000 TEUs.

Two regional ports—Kulhudhuffushi in the north and Hithadhoo in the south—have been commissioned for international service but are not active, because of lack of traffic. There are also a few proprietary port facilities/jetties at resort islands for receiving goods and passengers.

### Pakistan

Pakistan has three ports: Karachi, Port Qasim, and Gwadar. Karachi, the largest of the three, was opened in 1854 and handles most containers as well as bulks and general cargo. Port Qasim, about 40 kilometers from Karachi, was built in 1980. It was initially intended to specialize in bulks, but it now has one container terminal, opened in 1995, and a second container terminal is being built. The third port, Gwadar, opened in 2007, has attracted almost no cargo.[3]

Karachi handled 61 percent and Port Qasim 39 percent of Pakistan's throughput in 2012/13. In recent years both ports dredged their channels to accommodate ships with 13-meter drafts. The Karachi Port Trust is currently constructing a deep-water container terminal at the entrance to the port, with a water depth of 16–18 meters, to be operated by Hutchison Port Holdings.

### Sri Lanka

Sri Lanka has seven ports, with the Port of Colombo by far the most important. All of the country's container traffic flows through Colombo, a major international container transhipment hub: About 75 percent of its traffic consists of transhipment of other countries' containers.

The Port of Hambantota is being constructed. When completed, it will have two 100,000 deadweight ton (dwt) container berths and two 10,000 dwt feeder berths and will become the second-largest port in Sri Lanka. Sri Lanka's other ports—Galle, Kankasanturai, Oluvil, Point Pedro, and Trincomalee—are small and handle little commercial traffic.

## Policy and Institutional Framework

Like all transport sectors, the port sector is governed by a set of specialized institutions with different responsibilities and a framework of policies that guides the sector's functioning. The following subsections briefly describe the policy and institutional framework in the port sector in each South Asian country.

## Bangladesh

Chittagong and Mongla are managed by port authorities that report to the Ministry of Shipping, which provides overall sector policy guidance and some regulatory oversight. Both guidance and oversight are at best light touch. The Chittagong Port Authority exercises a high degree of operational and financial autonomy, although major expenditures require approval from the Ministry of Shipping.

## India

India's port structure is marked by the distinction between major and nonmajor ports (figure 1.4). The Indian Ports Act, 1908 defines the jurisdiction of the central and state government over ports. Major ports are placed under the Union list of the Indian Constitution and administered by the central government under the Indian Ports Act, 1908 and the Major Port Trust Act, 1963. Under the Major Port Trust Act, each major port is governed by a board of trustees appointed by the central government.

Of the 12 major ports, 11 are run by port trusts; the 12th, Ennore Port, is a corporation under the Companies Act.[4] For the ports governed by the board of trustees, the powers of these trustees are limited and bound by directions on policy matters and orders from the Ministry of Shipping, which has been entrusted with responsibility for formulating and implementing policies for major ports. Nonmajor ports are placed on the concurrent list of the Constitution and administered by state governments, under the Indian Ports Act. At the state level, the department in charge of ports or the State Maritime Board (created through state legislation) is responsible for formulating waterfront development policies and plans, regulating and overseeing the management of state ports, attracting private investment in the development of state ports, and enforcing environmental protection standards.

**Figure 1.4  Institutional Structure of India's Port Sector**

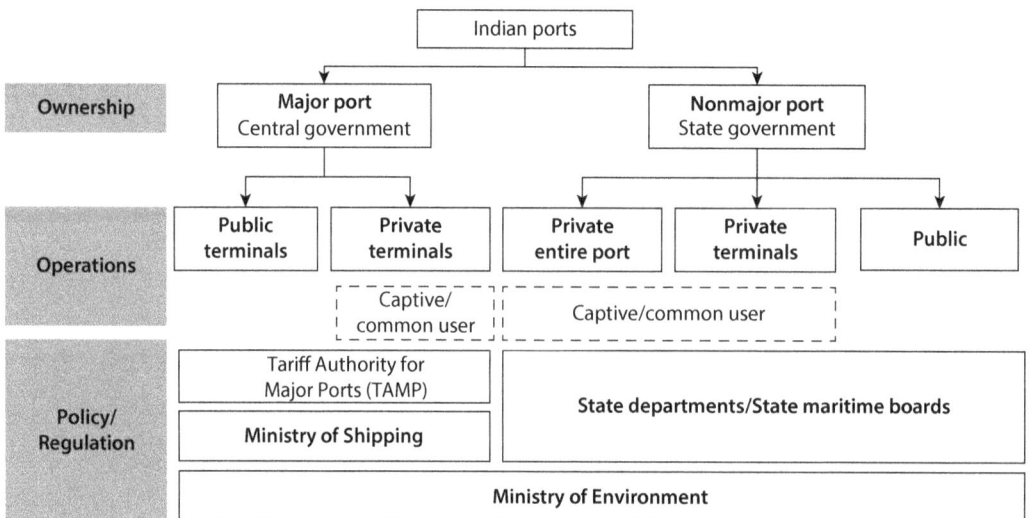

Major and nonmajor ports are subject to different regulatory regimes. Major ports are subject to tariff regulation via the Tariff Authority for Major Ports (TAMP); nonmajor ports are not. Overall, regulation of planning, investment, and tariff-setting is far more onerous for major ports than for nonmajor ports.

### Maldives

In 1986 a port authority–type organization was set up under the Ministry of Transport and Communication to own and operate the ports in Maldives. In 2008, however, commercial operations were transferred to a government-owned company, Maldives Ports Limited (MPL), leaving only the regulatory functions of the authority directly under the ministry. MPL, which has been corporatized, is managed by a board whose members are appointed by the president of Maldives; a managing director controls the day-to-day operations of the port. The ministry plays a key role in formulating sector policy and regulating the sector.

### Pakistan

The Ministry of Ports and Shipping functions as the central policy-making and administrative authority for Pakistan's port sector. Its main responsibility is to provide policy guidelines to the country's ports, which are run by port trusts/authorities.

A board of trustees, comprising a chairperson and 10 trustees, administers the Port of Karachi. The federal government appoints the chair, who is also the chief executive of the Karachi Port Trust. The remaining 10 trustees are distributed equally between the public and the private sectors.

An act of Parliament in 1973 established the Port Qasim Authority, under the administrative control of the Ministry of Ports and Shipping. The chair of its board is the chief executive of the port. The seven-person board includes members from both the public and the private sectors.

### Sri Lanka

The Sri Lanka Ports Authority (SLPA) was set up by an Act of Parliament in 1979 to administer and operate all commercial ports in the country. It ran all operations until 1999, when it started granting concessions for the operation of some container terminals.

The SLPA is also responsible for planning and tariffs. It sets its own tariffs and the tariffs in concession agreements, which are monitored by the Ministry of Ports and Aviation. The Ministry of Environment and Natural Resources and the Marine Pollution Prevention Authority regulate environmental matters at the port.

## Port Investments

Countries across the world have responded to the increase in container traffic with investments to expand the capacity of existing ports, introduce new technologies, and build entire new ports. This section shows the evolution of port investments at the regional and country levels during the past few decades.

### Regional Patterns

Private sector investment commitments in the port sector in all developing regions were significantly higher in 2000–14 than in 1990–99 (figure 1.5). The Private Participation in Infrastructure (PPI) database, a joint initiative of the World Bank and the Public-Private Infrastructure Advisory Facility (PPIAF), tracks private investment commitments for developing countries. It presents only partial investment information, as it does not include public investments. According to the PPI database, average annual investment commitments in ports in the developing world in 2000–14 were about 3.4 times those in 1990–99 (in current dollars). The number of new projects increased in all regions except Latin America and the Caribbean.

The South Asian port sector attracted significant interest from private investors in the late 2000s. During the 1990s the entire sector (container, bulk, and so forth) received 12 percent of private investment commitments in ports in the developing world, amounting to about $1.5 billion. This figure was far lower than the equivalent figures in East Asia ($6.1 billion) and Latin America and the Caribbean ($4.5 billion). Between 2000 and 2014, the South Asian port sector attracted $10 billion in private investment commitments (16 percent of all port commitments in the developing world). Two-thirds of the investment commitments during this period took place between 2006 and 2010, after the largest number of new projects reached financial closure in 2005 (figure 1.6).

**Figure 1.5  Private Sector Investment Commitments to Port Projects, by Region, 1990–99 and 2000–14**

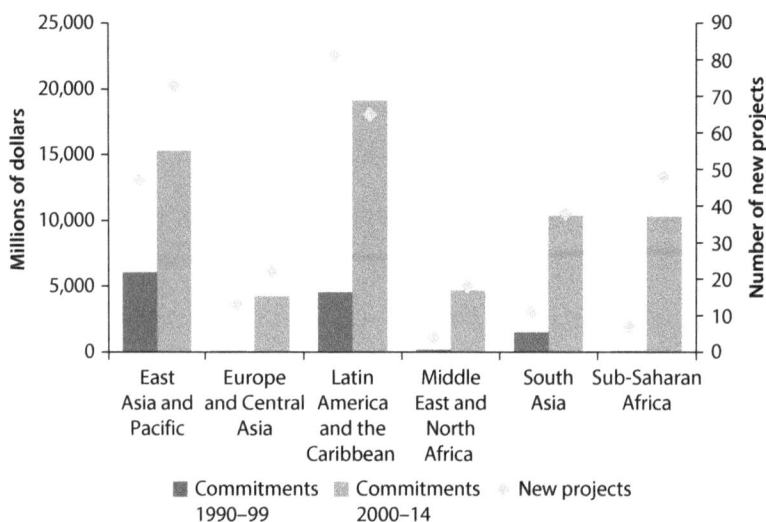

*Source:* PPI database.

Between 2000 and 2010, expansion of container port facilities was weak in South Asia (only Sub-Saharan Africa saw less expansion). Such expansion represents a good proxy for total investment in container ports. East Asia led the expansion during this period, particularly with respect to berth length (figure 1.7), thanks to the major expansion of container ports in China. Expansion, particularly of terminal area, was also strong in Latin America and the Caribbean. South Asia, led by India, and Eastern Europe and Central Asia, led by the Russian Federation and Turkey, experienced similar expansions of their container port facilities between 2000 and 2010.

**Figure 1.6  Annual Private Sector Investment Commitments to Port Projects in South Asia, 1995–2014**

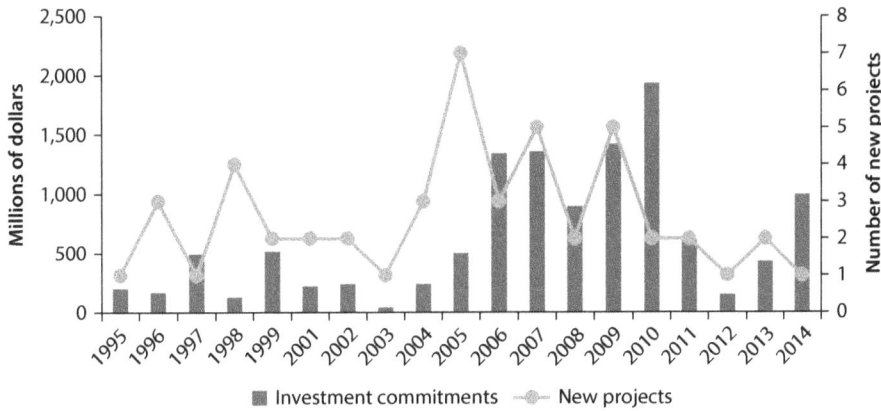

*Source:* PPI database.

**Figure 1.7  Container Port Facilities Added between 2000 and 2010, by Region**

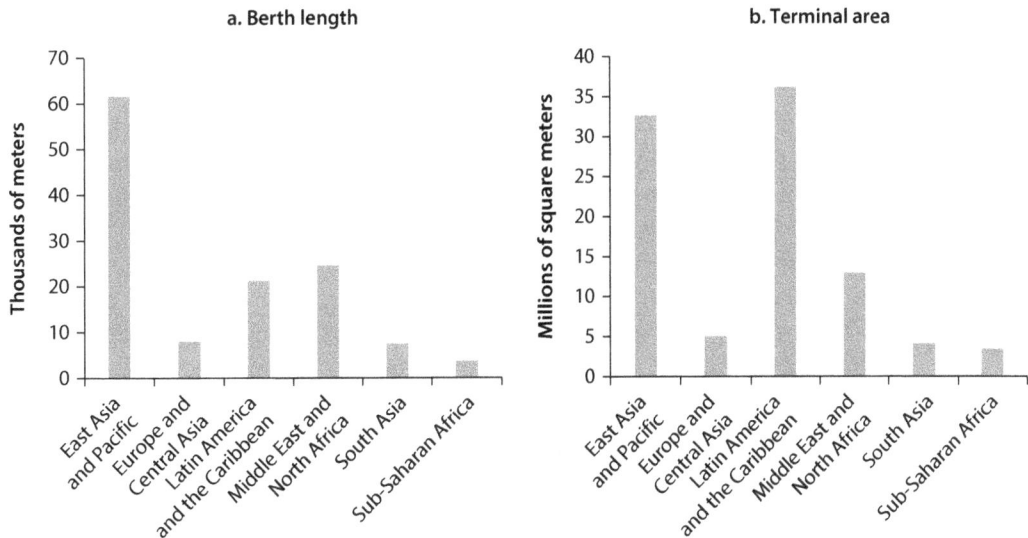

*Sources: Containerisation International Yearbook* 2002 and 2012.

### Country-Level Patterns

In the past two decades, the investment pattern in the port sector was not uniform across South Asia. India, Pakistan, and Sri Lanka took the lead, followed by Bangladesh and Maldives.

### Bangladesh

Development of port facilities at Chittagong, Bangladesh's largest port, has been slow. The Chittagong Port Authority (CPA) has completed only one fully special-ized terminal, the Chittagong Container Terminal, and it handles only a third of total traffic. Just over half of the port's container traffic is still handled at general cargo berths. The remaining containers are handled at the New Moorings Container Terminal, built in 2007, at a cost of $100 million, which still has no container cranes. Although occupancy at the CPA container berths is high and rising, there is a pressing need for more investment in capacity.

The Port of Mongla has had excess capacity for many years. There are five usable berths; another four remain unfinished. Two of the five are used for containers and general cargo, using ships' gear to load and unload. Occupancy is very low (14 percent at one berth, 37 percent at the other).

### India

The latest strategy for the Indian port sector—Maritime Agenda 2010–20 (Ministry of Shipping 2011) and Sagarmala (Ministry of Shipping 2016)—lays out the investment plan. The bulk of future investment is expected to go toward development of container and coal-handling capacity on the east coast and con-tainer-handling capacity on the west coast.

Leveraging private sector investment for port development is a key theme in India. By September 2013, 58 port projects with private investment were ongo-ing, for a total investment of $11 billion. Another 83 port projects with private investment were under consideration or in the initial stages, with total planned investment of $23 billion.

The port sector, which was traditionally capacity constrained, witnessed rapid growth in capacity and volume of throughput (figure 1.8) following reforms that began in the late 1990s (figure 1.9). Capacity additions and the slowdown in the growth of traffic after 2008 created a gap between supply and demand. Almost 20 years of experience and experimentation with reforms has led to an improved investment environment, which is necessary to ensure that growth is supported and facilitated.

The two largest container ports in India are in the midst of expanding their container capacity. In early 2014 JNPT, historically the largest container port in India, awarded a concession to PSA International Pte Ltd. (PSA) to develop and operate its fourth container terminal. When finished, this terminal will have annual capacity of 4.8 million TEUs, more than doubling JNPT's current capac-ity of 4.1 million TEUs.

Mundra is the most dynamic container port in India, consistently growing at almost 35 percent a year since it began operating its first container terminal, in 2003.

**Figure 1.8  Annual Capacity and Volume of Throughput at All Ports and Major Ports in India, 1998–2013**

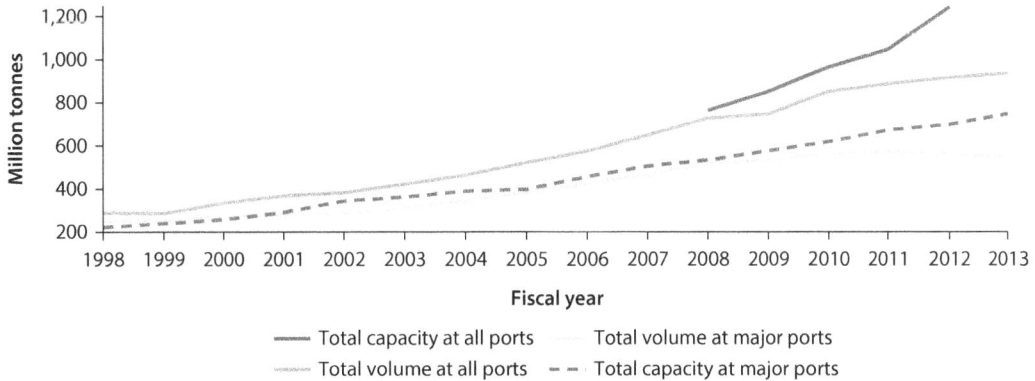

*Source:* Ministry of Road Transport and Highways of India 2014.

In mid-2014 Adani Ports and Special Economic Zone (APSEZ), the parent company of the Port of Mundra, signed an agreement with CMA CGM S.A. (CMA CGM) for the development of the fourth container terminal, which will add 1.3 million TEUs of annual capacity.

### Maldives

Relatively little development has occurred at the Port of Malé. In 2006 the government requested PPIAF assistance in selecting the location of a new port and choosing the optimal form of public-private partnerships to implement the project. Following PPIAF technical assistance, the government opted for Thilafushi, on a build-operate-transfer (BOT) basis. The procurement process was put in place by the government and the bidding was expected in 2012, but it has not yet taken place.

There have been some improvements at Malé North Harbour, where about 40 percent of imports are reshipped to outer atolls. Congestion had been a problem for ship operators, cargo handlers, and ship owners. With Asian Development Bank (ADB) assistance in 2011, berth length was more than doubled.

Island harbors have been developed to improve access, but maintenance of government ports, jetties, and breakwaters on the islands suffers from neglect. Their maintenance is the responsibility of island development committees, which have neither the resources to maintain them nor the authority to levy fees for their upkeep. When these facilities are damaged or destroyed, it is therefore necessary to call on the central government to repair or replace them.

### Pakistan

Capacity at Pakistani ports has been consistently adequate over the past 20 years. At Karachi three container terminals were developed, partly through private sector investment. The Karachi International Container Terminal was completed in 1998, and the Pakistan International Container Terminal was completed in 2004, each at a cost of about $150 million. The South Asia Pakistan Terminal, which will begin

**Figure 1.9 Key Events in the Evolution of the Policy and Regulatory Framework for Ports in India**

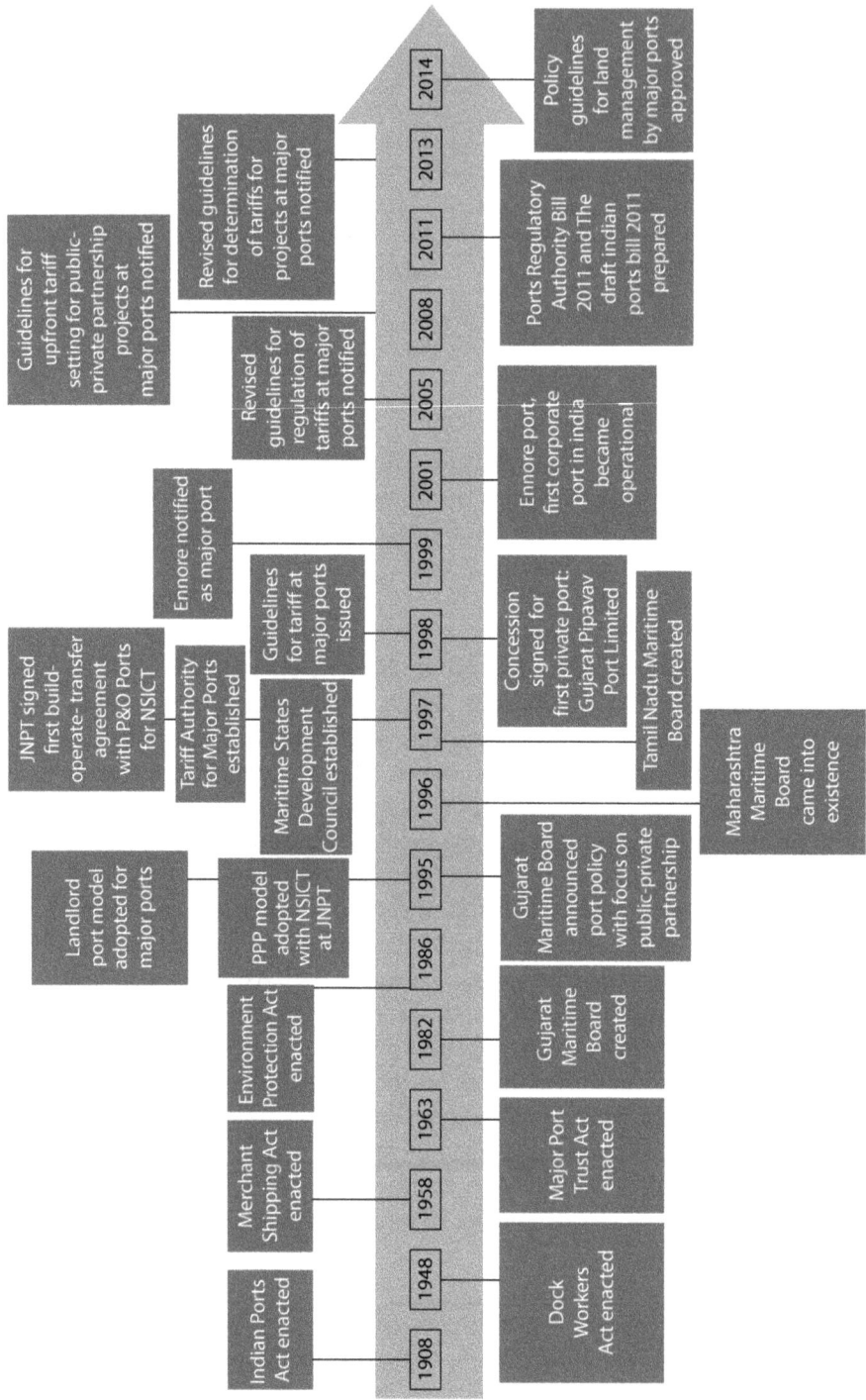

*Sources:* Data from the Ministry of Shipping, Government of India, and Indian Ports Association.
*Note:* JNPT = Jawaharlal Nehru Port; NSICT = Nhava Sheva International Container Terminal.

operations in mid-2016, will cost about $1 billion. It will have four berths at 16 meters depth extendable to 18 meters, with a quay wall of 1,500 meters.

Mechanization of bulk handling and the decline of break bulk have meant that the capacity of noncontainer berths has also increased. Berth occupancy is currently low, because of the recent decline in noncontainer traffic. In 2013 berth occupancy was 54 percent at the Karachi International Container Terminal and 62 percent at the Pakistan International Container Terminal. At Port Qasim the private sector or local industries funded the container and most other terminals; berth occupancies are reasonable. Port Gwadar, which opened in 2007, was funded by the Chinese government and is operated by the state-run China Overseas Port Holding Company (COPHC).

### Sri Lanka

Major port investment at Colombo has been determined by transshipment traffic. Stagnation of traffic in the late 1990s, as a result of high costs and low productivity, led the government to seek proposals from investors to develop the port in conjunction with the SLPA. The South Asia Gateway Terminal submitted the only bid. Construction of the terminal started in 1999, under a concession agreement with the SLPA to expand an existing general cargo quay into a modern container terminal. Its capacity was originally estimated at 1.1 million TEU, although it was soon handling much more. The construction costs of about $154 million were well below the original budget of $246 million.

The next major expansion at Colombo was the construction of the South Harbour. Planning started in 2003, and operations started in 2014. The terminal is run by Colombo International Container Terminal (CICT), which invested $500 million to construct and operate the Colombo South Container Terminal for 35 years, after which the terminal will be handed over to the SLPA. The terminal has an estimated capacity of 2.4 million TEUs. Two other terminals with the same capacity are planned in subsequent phases. The South Harbour development received support from the Asian Development Bank for the breakwater, through a $400 million loan.

The first major project outside Colombo is the Port of Hambantota, where China Merchants Holdings (CMHI) and the China Harbour Engineering Company are building a new terminal, at a cost of $600 million.[5] It is expected that the Chinese company will hold a majority share of the joint venture with SLPA. The first phase of the new port was completed in 2010. It is currently intended mainly for break-bulk cargo, vehicles, and liquid cargo, but SLPA intends to develop it as an alternate port to Colombo, with the second phase including a container terminal.

## Tariffs

Global experience of successful ports suggests favoring the market setting of tariffs through competition, including internationally competitive tenders (competition for the port), interport competition (competition between ports)

Competitiveness of South Asia's Container Ports • http://dx.doi.org/10.1596/978-1-4648-0892-0

and intraport competition (competition among multiple operators at the same port). However, price controls are often a part of port concessions and contracts.

South Asia's experience has been mixed and at times run against the tide of reform. In Bangladesh and Sri Lanka, the port authority sets tariffs, which are subject to oversight by the Ministry of Shipping. Colombo's focus on transshipment exposes the port to high levels of price competition, as it is forced to compete with larger and better-positioned competitors. However, controls do exist to balance competitive forces among terminals. In Maldives the Ministry of Transport and Communications sets tariffs directly. In Pakistan the Ministry of Ports and Shipping sets tariffs directly.

In India the major ports typically offer terminals within the ports to private developers, selected through an open competitive bidding process. The Tariff Authority for Major Ports (TAMP) regulates tariffs at these terminals. The state maritime agency offers nonmajor ports to private developers for sites on a concession basis, with flexibility on tariffs and development plans. The asymmetric regulation of major and nonmajor ports creates an uneven playing field tilted in favor of nonmajor ports. Recent evidence indicates that nonmajor ports are rapidly ramping up their cargo whereas major ports are subject to delays in expanding capacity. TAMP is empowered to notify not only the rates but also the conditionality governing application of the rates. Guidelines issued in 2008 establish a tariff cap, which is set upfront, before inviting bids for a public-private partnership (PPP) project (TAMP 2008). With respect to tariff increases of existing terminals, a cost-plus approach is applied, per guidelines set in 2005 (TAMP 2005).

India's Planning Commission has discussed the tariff-setting issue. A 2010 report on the port sector observed that tariff-setting by TAMP sometimes led to delays that slowed the procurement process of PPP projects (Government of India 2010). The report also noted that performance standards used by TAMP for tariff-setting and those agreed to by the parties in concession agreements could differ. The committee that issued the report proposed gradual policy changes that could eventually lead to tariffs being set by market forces.

South Asian port tariffs are competitive. Table 1.1 compares terminal handling charges at selected ports. In order to compete for transshipment traffic, which is very sensitive to prices, Colombo charges much lower tariffs for transshipment traffic ($37 per TEU) than for Sri Lankan imports and exports ($151 per TEU). The high charges for Sri Lankan containers result in a terminal handling charge imposed by the shipping lines that is higher than the charges of other subcontinent ports. Colombo and the main South Asian ports still charge competitive tariffs, however.

An exception is Malé, where as a consequence of inefficiencies and high manning levels, handing charges total about $415 per TEU. Malé shares similarities with many of the smaller Caribbean islands that are dependent on tourism and have limited traffic. Like ports in those countries, it is run by the state and overmanned (thanks to protection by local unions) and has low productivity, high costs, and high tariffs.

**Table 1.1  Terminal Handling Charges at Selected Ports, May 2015**
*dollars/TEU*

| Port | Charge |
| --- | --- |
| Chennai | 65 |
| Chittagong | 85 |
| JNPT | 95 |
| Karachi and Qasim | 115 |
| Mundra | 116 |
| Colombo | 151 |
| Singapore | 161 |
| Salalah | 194 |
| Dubai | 215 |
| Rotterdam | 268 |
| Los Angeles | 390 |
| Malé | 415 |

*Sources:* www.safmarine.com and port authorities.
*Note:* The terminal handling charge is the charge to the shipping lines' customers that is supposed to cover the container-handling charges paid to the ports plus minor additional costs.

## Concluding Remarks

The container port industry has become increasingly competitive in terms of the hinterlands served, the shipping lines it attracts, and the transshipment roles it performs. South Asian port tariffs are competitive, but port tariffs account for only a small share of overall trade costs. The indirect costs associated with delays, and inefficiencies play a more significant role in shippers' port choices.

As container traffic keeps growing and physical expansion is constrained by the limited supply of available land around most ports, port facilities will need to become more productive if they are to remain competitive. How to improve productivity to accommodate the anticipated increase in container traffic presents a challenge to port operators and port authorities (Le-Griffin and Murphy 2006). Assessing how ports perform is useful not only for transport planning but also for informing port management, policy, and regulation. The next chapter presents a comprehensive assessment of the performance of South Asian container ports.

## Notes

1. The TEU is a unit of cargo capacity often used to describe the capacity of container ships and container terminals. It is based on the volume of a 20-foot-long intermodal container, a standard-sized metal box that can be easily transferred across different modes of transportation, such as ships, trains, and trucks.

2. There has been much discussion about constructing a deep-water port in Sonadia, south of Chittagong. A feasibility study was completed in 2009, and the government received offers of assistance from companies in China, the United Arab Emirates, and the Netherlands in 2013. Although discussions have taken place at the highest level of government, no decision has yet been made on whether the project will proceed.

3. The port is located in the desert, about 530 kilometers from the main coastal center of economic activity around Karachi. It has very limited road or rail links with the country's other main areas of economic activity, which are about 1,000–1,500 kilometers inland from all three of the main ports.

4. Ennore Port, which handled only one container vessel in 2009/10, is not considered a container port in the context of this report, although it plans to become an important player in the container sector in the near future. In 2014 the port awarded APSEZ a concession to design, build, finance, operate, and transfer a container terminal with container capacity of 1.4 million TEUs. The first phase is expected to be operational by 2016/17.

5. The first traffic arrived in 2012, but the port is not yet finished.

## References

Government of India. 2010. *Report of the Committee under the Chairmanship of Shri BK Chaturvedi.* September, New Delhi.

Le-Griffin, H. D., and M. Murphy. 2006. "Container Terminal Productivity: Experiences at the Ports of Los Angeles and Long Beach." Presentation at the National Urban Freight Conference, Long Beach, CA, February.

Lloyd's List. 2002–12. *Containerisation International Yearbook.* London.

Ministry of Road Transport and Highways. 2014. *Basic Port Statistics of India.* Transport Research Wing, Government of India, New Delhi.

Ministry of Shipping. 2011. *Maritime Agenda 2010–2020.* Government of India. http://shipping.nic.in/showfile.php?lid=261.

———. 2016. *Sagarmala: Building Gateways of Growth.* National Perspective Plan. Government of India. http://shipmin.nic.in/showfile.php?lid=2217.

TAMP (Tariff Authority for Major Ports). 2005. *Guidelines for Regulation of Tariff at Major Ports.* http://www.tariffauthority.gov.in/htmldocs/orders/guidelines/rev-guideline.pdf.

———. 2008. *Guidelines for Upfront Tariff Setting for PPP Projects at Major Port Trusts.* http://www.tariffauthority.gov.in/htmldocs/orders/guidelines/guidelines08.pdf.

CHAPTER 2

# Performance of South Asian Container Ports

## Introduction

In recent years the global container port industry transitioned from a public management environment with very limited competition, in which most ports enjoyed monopoly control over the handling of cargoes from their hinterland, to an environment with increasing private participation and competition (Coelli and others 2003; Cullinane and Song 2006). Beginning in the late 1990s/early 2000s, India, Pakistan, and Sri Lanka reformed their port sectors, introducing private sector participation through implementation of the "landlord" port model (box 3.1 describes all port models). Bangladesh is the only country on the Indian subcontinent that has not adopted this model. The desire to create a competitive environment now prevails in the port industry. More container ports need to ensure that they can physically handle cargo and successfully compete for it.

Where competition is limited, the search for efficiency gains is at the core of the regulation debate. Performance analyses have become well established and informative tools for economic regulation in infrastructure industries and to some extent the port industry (Defilippi 2010; Defilippi and Flor 2008; Estache, Tovar, and Trujillo 2004; World Bank 2007).[1]

A port can be seen as the collection of processes that is needed to bring its outputs to customers (Talley 2012). Although it would be ideal to evaluate a port based on a single measure of performance, doing so is not feasible, because a port's overall performance depends on the performance of each of these processes and the interactions among these processes.

The three main angles for evaluating port performance are operational, economic, and financial. The operational perspective refers to the quality of the outputs provided, which in the case of ports refers to the time it takes to provide ship-related port services and the intensity of use of the port's facilities. The economic angle takes into account factors such as the mix of inputs used, the technology used to transform inputs into outputs, and the port's productive scale. The financial perspective addresses the mix of financial resources and profitability indicators.

Studies on the economic performance of the port industry are relatively new, with the first studies dating from the mid-1990s.[2] Other infrastructure and service sectors (electricity, water, sanitation, banking, health), including other transport sectors, such as railways and airports, have benefited from a more extensive literature on efficiency and productivity. The change in the competitive environment is partly responsible for the increasing interest in economic performance studies in the late 1990s and early 2000s.

This chapter presents a comprehensive assessment of the operational and economic performance of South Asian container ports. The first section assesses the operational performance of ports since 2000, based on a set of time-based measures. The second section analyzes economic performance by benchmarking South Asian ports against one another and against other ports in the Indian and Western Pacific Oceans. The last section offers some concluding remarks.

## Operational Performance

Port tariffs are an important factor in port competitiveness, but they account for a small share of overall trade costs (Tongzon 1995). The indirect costs associated with delays, loss of markets and customer confidence, and opportunities forgone because of inefficient service play a more significant role in shippers' port choices.

The port industry has traditionally relied on time-based partial indicators to assess performance. Port authorities use these indicators to assess port operations and plan future development.

This section examines the total time ships spend at port, in order to identify the main bottlenecks. The analysis is based on the most exhaustive database on time statistics on South Asian ports, collated using the Basic Port Statistics of India for 1999–2014 and data provided by port authorities in Bangladesh, Pakistan, and Sri Lanka.

Four metrics are used:

- Average turnaround time (TAT) is the number of days ships spend at port, from arrival and offloading to uploading and departure.
- Average preberthing waiting time (WT) is the number of days a ship has to wait before it can dock.
- Average percentage of idle time at berth (IT) is the time a ship is at berth but not receiving any services as a share of the total time it spends at berth.
- Average percentage of nonidle time at berth (NIT) is the time a ship is at berth and being serviced as a share of the total time it spends at berth.

Figure 2.1 provides a graphical representation of the time structure considered in the analysis.

**Figure 2.1  Schematic of Port Operations and Performance Indicators**

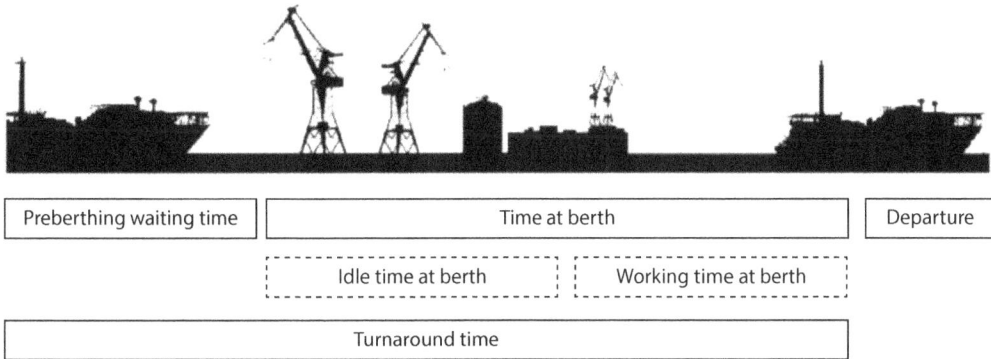

| Preberthing waiting time | Time at berth | Departure |

| Idle time at berth | Working time at berth |

| Turnaround time |

**Figure 2.2  Breakdown of Average Time Spent at South Asian Container Ports, 2000 and 2012**

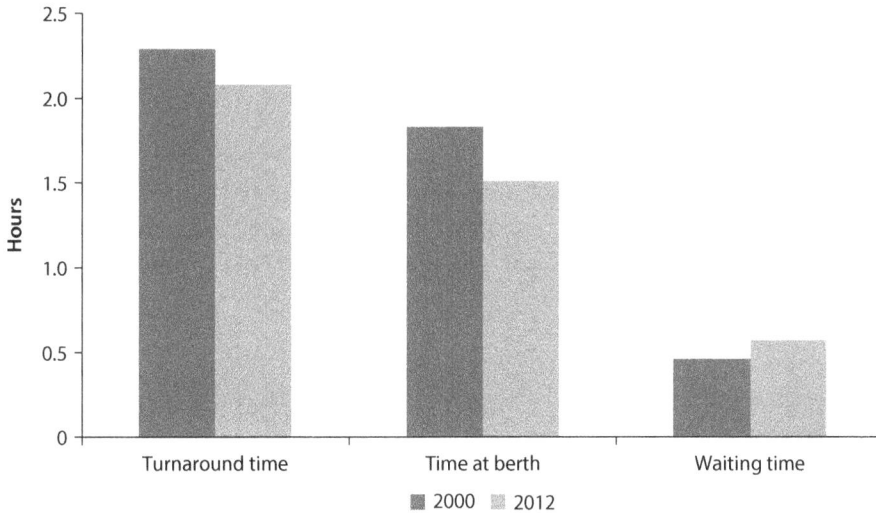

■ 2000    ▒ 2012

*Sources:* Ministry of Road Transport and Highways of India 2014 and port authorities' websites.

## Performance within South Asia

Average vessel turnaround time in South Asian container ports declined between 2000 and 2012, falling from about 2.3 days to about 2.1 days (figure 2.2). Marked improvement occurred in the early 2000s, but it was partially offset later in the decade.

The averages mask wide regional variations. Vessel turnaround in Chittagong (Bangladesh) and Kolkata (India) takes much longer than average in most years (more than four days). In contrast, ships spend only slightly more than a day at Colombo or Cochin. Although intraregional differences are large, the decrease in turnaround time was accompanied by a convergence in turnaround time, with the standard deviation falling from 1.2 in 2000 to 0.96 in 2012.

Average preberth waiting times increased between 2000 and 2012, implying that capacity did not expand as much as needed to avoid increasing congestion. Many factors, including ship sizes, berth capacity, and operational efficiency, affect preberthing waiting time, which increased from 0.46 days in 2000 to 0.57 in 2012, having spiked as high as 0.76 in 2010 (figure 2.3). Whatever the collective causes, increasing waiting time connotes a deteriorating situation.

Table 2.1 shows the average annual preberthing waiting time in South Asian container ports between 2000 and 2012. Although waiting times declined at some ports (for example, Chennai), they increased at most ports, with times at Kandla, JNPT, and Cochin rising most.

Ports have offset the increasing preberth waiting time by improving the efficiency of their operations at the berthing stage. The average time ships spent at berth fell from 1.83 days in 2000 to 1.51 days in 2012. The average proportion of time ships were not being serviced while at berth (idle time at berth) fell from 23 percent to 19 percent. The decline in the share of idle time was most marked at Chittagong and Visakhapatnam; at only a few ports, such as Kandla, did the share of idle time increase. Karachi and Colombo have always had relatively low idle time ratios. The increasing prevalence of larger vessel visits could explain the pattern observed at Colombo and JNPT, where the time spent at berth increased even as the share of idle time decreased significantly.

The evolution of average turnaround time by country shows that South Asia comprises two very different realities, with Pakistan and Sri Lanka performing better than India and Bangladesh in terms of time efficiency (figure 2.4). India is gradually losing competitiveness in terms of time, after improving at the beginning of the decade.

**Figure 2.3  Average Preberthing Waiting Time at South Asian Container Ports, 2000–12**

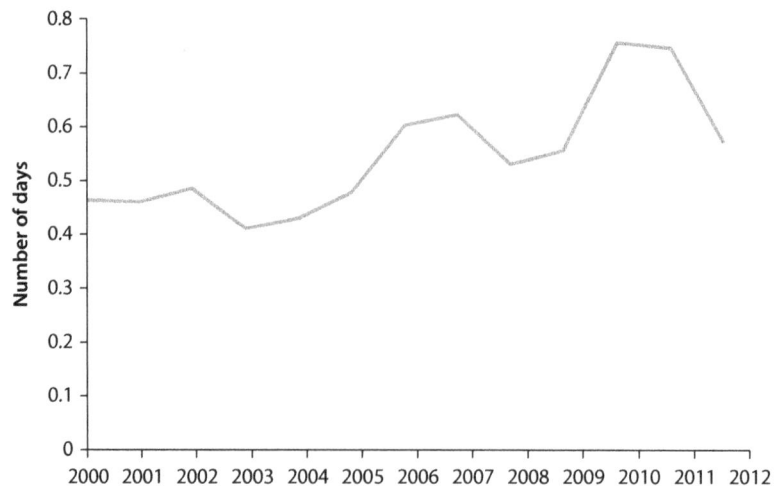

*Sources:* Ministry of Road Transport and Highways of India 2014 and port authorities' websites.

**Table 2.1 Annual Average Operational Performance of South Asia's Container Ports, 2000–12**

| Port/indicator | 2000 | 2001 | 2002 | 2003 | 2004 | 2005 | 2006 | 2007 | 2008 | 2009 | 2010 | 2011 | 2012 |
|---|---|---|---|---|---|---|---|---|---|---|---|---|---|
| **Chennai** | | | | | | | | | | | | | |
| TAT (days) | 3.90 | 6.95 | 2.15 | 1.36 | 2.64 | 1.38 | 1.51 | 2.48 | 2.03 | 1.74 | 1.73 | 2.46 | 1.83 |
| WT (days) | 1.30 | 1.29 | 0.73 | 0.34 | 0.90 | 0.25 | 0.27 | 0.88 | 0.57 | 0.48 | 0.37 | 0.68 | 0.35 |
| IT (percent) | 25.0 | — | — | 2.3 | 33.2 | — | — | — | 0.0 | 14.7 | — | — | — |
| **Chittagong** | | | | | | | | | | | | | |
| TAT (days) | — | — | 4.56 | 4.30 | 3.99 | 4.08 | 7.10 | 5.02 | 2.48 | 2.48 | 4.31 | 3.21 | 3.23 |
| WT (days) | — | — | 1.06 | 1.18 | 0.78 | 1.40 | 3.27 | 1.94 | 0.47 | 0.46 | 1.44 | 0.74 | 0.57 |
| IT (percent) | — | — | — | — | — | 32.3 | 37.6 | 10.5 | 10.5 | 10.9 | 8.7 | 7.7 | 8.6 |
| **Cochin** | | | | | | | | | | | | | |
| TAT (days) | 2.00 | 1.97 | 2.06 | 1.61 | 2.23 | 1.67 | 1.14 | 1.14 | 1.37 | 1.45 | 1.78 | 0.96 | 0.73 |
| WT (days) | 0.40 | 0.38 | 0.51 | 0.29 | 0.33 | 0.35 | 0.29 | 0.55 | 0.88 | 0.89 | 0.97 | 0.98 | 1.03 |
| IT (percent) | 30.0 | 24.8 | 21.3 | 20.3 | 20.3 | — | — | 10.0 | 10.0 | 10.0 | 39.6 | 27.5 | 36.3 |
| **Colombo** | | | | | | | | | | | | | |
| TAT (days) | 0.77 | 0.87 | 0.66 | 0.53 | 0.56 | 0.57 | 0.72 | 0.79 | 0.86 | 0.79 | 1.04 | 0.95 | 0.86 |
| WT (days) | 0.11 | 0.13 | 0.08 | 0.06 | 0.05 | 0.03 | 0.08 | 0.11 | 0.19 | 0.16 | 0.28 | 0.14 | 0.09 |
| IT (percent) | 12.4 | 10.9 | 9.6 | 9.2 | 8.2 | 7.5 | 6.4 | 6.1 | 4.7 | 7.9 | 7.1 | 6.1 | 6.9 |
| **Haldia** | | | | | | | | | | | | | |
| TAT (days) | 2.10 | 2.54 | 2.24 | 2.10 | 2.18 | 2.12 | 1.82 | 2.34 | 2.47 | 2.56 | 2.90 | 2.43 | 2.20 |
| WT (days) | 0.10 | 0.10 | 0.31 | 0.26 | 0.29 | 0.39 | 0.47 | 1.02 | 0.90 | 1.13 | 1.33 | 0.70 | 0.69 |
| IT (percent) | 30.0 | 27.7 | 32.5 | 29.5 | 28.4 | 29.8 | 42.6 | 36.7 | 28.9 | 27.9 | 26.9 | 28.7 | 28.7 |
| **JNPT** | | | | | | | | | | | | | |
| TAT (days) | 1.10 | 2.46 | 1.73 | 1.71 | 1.58 | 1.74 | 1.25 | 1.69 | 1.62 | 1.45 | 1.92 | 1.77 | 2.02 |
| WT (days) | 0.40 | 0.38 | 0.32 | 0.55 | 0.56 | 0.79 | 0.51 | 0.82 | 0.79 | 0.57 | 0.95 | 0.83 | 0.96 |
| IT (percent) | 36.0 | 7.9 | 11.4 | 13.0 | 3.7 | 4.4 | 5.6 | 6.5 | 6.6 | 7.7 | 10.6 | 26.6 | 8.1 |
| **Kandla** | | | | | | | | | | | | | |
| TAT (days) | 2.50 | 2.53 | 2.21 | 2.18 | 2.76 | 2.42 | 2.30 | 1.76 | 2.66 | 1.71 | 2.17 | 3.00 | 3.00 |
| WT (days) | 0.60 | 0.55 | 0.60 | 0.50 | 0.71 | 0.59 | 0.56 | 0.42 | 0.57 | 0.56 | 0.76 | 1.38 | 0.89 |
| IT (percent) | 19.0 | 16.0 | 15.7 | 13.3 | 12.3 | 14.6 | 12.0 | 19.1 | 46.2 | 33.4 | 24.6 | 25.0 | 28.0 |
| **Karachi** | | | | | | | | | | | | | |
| TAT (days) | 1.67 | 1.58 | 1.71 | 1.58 | 1.58 | 1.54 | 1.54 | 1.58 | 1.54 | 1.63 | 1.58 | 1.50 | 1.45 |
| WT (days) | 0.29 | 0.31 | 0.31 | 0.32 | 0.33 | 0.32 | 0.29 | 0.31 | 0.50 | 0.50 | 0.50 | 0.42 | 0.29 |
| IT (percent) | 9.1 | 9.1 | 9.1 | 9.5 | 4.3 | 4.5 | 4.8 | 4.8 | 4.3 | 9.1 | 4.0 | 4.6 | 4.8 |
| **Kolkata** | | | | | | | | | | | | | |
| TAT (days) | 4.60 | 3.68 | 3.56 | 3.04 | 3.07 | 3.09 | 3.29 | 4.53 | 3.86 | 4.55 | 4.45 | 4.21 | 3.93 |
| WT (days) | 0.50 | 0.50 | 0.51 | 0.42 | 0.28 | 0.36 | 0.36 | 0.45 | 0.41 | 0.56 | 0.67 | 0.61 | 0.44 |
| IT (percent) | 31.0 | 33.0 | 31.4 | 26.8 | 23.9 | 28.4 | 31.1 | 30.1 | 31.8 | 29.9 | 27.8 | 22.1 | 22.6 |
| **Mumbai** | | | | | | | | | | | | | |
| TAT (days) | 3.80 | 3.60 | 3.30 | 2.48 | 2.66 | 2.54 | 2.43 | 2.34 | 2.59 | 2.85 | 3.28 | 4.72 | 2.57 |
| WT (days) | 0.60 | 0.62 | 0.69 | 0.41 | 0.48 | 0.71 | 0.65 | 0.39 | 0.51 | 0.70 | 0.96 | 1.25 | 0.47 |
| IT (percent) | 24.0 | 26.4 | 22.5 | 19.8 | 17.5 | 22.0 | 20.9 | 24.4 | 15.4 | 35.9 | 22.0 | 25.9 | 27.2 |

*table continues next page*

**Table 2.1  Annual Average Operational Performance of South Asia's Container Ports, 2000–12** *(continued)*

| Port/indicator | 2000 | 2001 | 2002 | 2003 | 2004 | 2005 | 2006 | 2007 | 2008 | 2009 | 2010 | 2011 | 2012 |
|---|---|---|---|---|---|---|---|---|---|---|---|---|---|
| **Tuticorin** | | | | | | | | | | | | | |
| TAT *(days)* | 1.00 | 0.96 | 1.08 | 1.11 | 1.12 | 1.02 | 1.08 | 1.23 | 1.20 | 1.38 | 1.70 | 1.54 | 1.68 |
| WT *(days)* | 0.50 | 0.53 | 0.58 | 0.52 | 0.43 | 0.47 | 0.42 | 0.46 | 0.44 | 0.56 | 0.61 | 0.43 | 0.54 |
| IT *(percent)* | 2.0 | 25.2 | 19.7 | 17.2 | 11.2 | 10.0 | 7.4 | 0.0 | 4.8 | 2.7 | 1.2 | 1.1 | — |
| **Visakhapatnam** | | | | | | | | | | | | | |
| TAT *(days)* | 1.80 | 1.65 | 1.16 | 0.60 | 0.43 | 0.55 | 0.57 | 0.74 | 0.73 | 0.83 | 1.12 | 1.95 | 1.51 |
| WT *(days)* | 0.30 | 0.28 | 0.13 | 0.09 | 0.03 | 0.08 | 0.07 | 0.13 | 0.14 | 0.11 | 0.25 | 0.81 | 0.54 |
| IT *(percent)* | 31.0 | 31.8 | 25.4 | 27.9 | 27.3 | 35.9 | 28.0 | 28.3 | 26.9 | 21.2 | 21.5 | 17.3 | 15.6 |
| **South Asia** | | | | | | | | | | | | | |
| TAT *(days)* | 2.29 | 2.62 | 2.20 | 1.88 | 2.07 | 1.89 | 2.06 | 2.14 | 1.95 | 1.95 | 2.33 | 2.39 | 2.08 |
| WT *(days)* | 0.46 | 0.46 | 0.49 | 0.41 | 0.43 | 0.48 | 0.60 | 0.62 | 0.53 | 0.56 | 0.76 | 0.75 | 0.57 |
| IT *(percent)* | 22.7 | 21.3 | 19.9 | 17.2 | 17.3 | 18.9 | 19.6 | 17.7 | 17.3 | 17.6 | 17.6 | 17.5 | 18.7 |

*Sources:* Ministry of Road Transport and Highways of India 2014 and port authorities' websites.
*Note:* The Port of Kolkata has two dock systems: Kolkata Docks at Kolkata and Haldia Dock Complex at Haldia. The measures for Kolkata and Haldia refer to the respective docks. TAT = average turnaround time; WT = average preberthing waiting time; IT = average idle time at berth; — = not available.

**Figure 2.4  Average Turnaround Time at South Asian Container Ports, by Country, 2000–12**

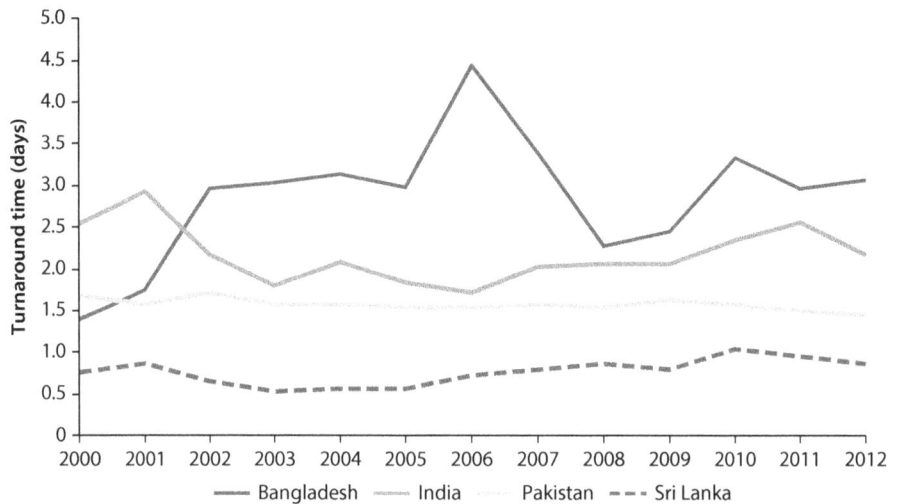

*Sources:* Ministry of Road Transport and Highways of India 2014 and port authorities' websites.

In summary, average turnaround time decreased between 2000 and 2012, as a result of increases in efficiency that offset the increase in congestion. The average share of idle time at berth fell, although there is still room for improvement.

### Performance across Regions

The Organisation for Economic Co-operation and Development (Ducruet, Itoh, and Merk 2014) developed an international comparison of average turnaround times, based on data from Lloyd's List Intelligence for the months of May 1996, 2006, and 2011.[3] Table 2.2 presents the main results.

Despite improvements, South Asian container ports fell farther behind best international performance between 2006 and 2011. Most regions experienced remarkable improvement in operational performance between 1996 and 2011. Asia as a whole improved to levels similar to levels in Europe and North America. In contrast, performance in South Asia worsened, with its average turnaround time increasing from 2.06 days in 2006 to 2.39 days in 2011 (table 2.1). This relative deterioration was driven by results at certain ports in India and Bangladesh. There was some convergence in the time ports take to service a ship, but no port in South Asia came close to the most competitive container ports worldwide, such as Singapore (0.5 days), Hong Kong (0.72 days), and Shanghai (0.79 days).

## Economic Performance

This section examines the economic performance—the process through which ports transform inputs (capital, labor, and land) into outputs. The key concepts are productivity and efficiency. Productivity examines the relationship between inputs and outputs in a given production process (Coelli and others 2005). It is the ratio of outputs to inputs. Changes in port productivity may come from efficiency improvements and technical changes. Technical changes can occur through, for example, new cargo handling equipment. Efficiency improvements can materialize through pure efficiency and scale efficiency.[4] Improvements in pure efficiency require improving the use of inputs (berths, cranes, labor)—by improving workers' ability to use new and sophisticated equipment, for example.

**Table 2.2  Container Port Turnaround Time, by Region, 1996, 2006, and 2011**

| Year/statistic (days) | Africa | Asia | Europe | Latin America | Middle East | North America | Oceania | All |
|---|---|---|---|---|---|---|---|---|
| **1996** | | | | | | | | |
| Average | 2.03 | 4.17 | 2.72 | 1.53 | 1.21 | 2.47 | 1.85 | 2.62 |
| Standard deviation | 2.60 | 10.95 | 8.10 | 1.78 | 0.81 | 3.02 | 2.82 | 7.13 |
| Maximum | 16 | 114 | 90 | 9 | 3 | 13 | 16.67 | 114 |
| **2006** | | | | | | | | |
| Average | 4.22 | 4.44 | 2.08 | 1.92 | 2.35 | 2.93 | 1.46 | 2.94 |
| Standard deviation | 5.91 | 10.11 | 5.00 | 2.30 | 3.70 | 6.13 | 2.02 | 6.62 |
| Maximum | 27 | 84 | 38 | 13 | 18.6 | 31.20 | 11 | 84 |
| **2011** | | | | | | | | |
| Average | 2.54 | 1.45 | 1.08 | 1.32 | 1.75 | 1.12 | 1.24 | 1.40 |
| Standard deviation | 1.58 | 1.59 | 1.06 | 1.11 | 1.50 | 0.70 | 0.80 | 1.34 |
| Maximum | 8.50 | 9.50 | 9.59 | 8.57 | 7.69 | 3.12 | 3.83 | 9.59 |

*Source:* Ducruet, Itoh, and Merk (2014).

Competitiveness of South Asia's Container Ports • http://dx.doi.org/10.1596/978-1-4648-0892-0

Improvements in scale efficiency occur if an increase (decrease) in the scale of the port is accompanied by a more (less) than proportional increase (decrease) in its outputs.[5]

### Methodological Framework

This section (based on Serebrisky 2012) reflects the latest developments in the literature on the computation of best practice frontiers. To the extent possible, the intuition behind the analysis is laid out with graphical representations of theoretical concepts.[6]

Partial performance indicators are easy to understand and calculate, but they do not provide a comprehensive picture of productivity and efficiency in an industry as complex as the port industry. To overcome the shortcomings of partial performance indicators, academics developed aggregate measures and estimation techniques based on the computation of best practice frontiers.

Efficiency analysis provides valuable information on whether a port or terminal is employing its inputs appropriately, making proper use of investments. Various methodologies have been developed, ranging from those that estimate efficiency through econometric models (parametric approach) to those that make use of mathematical programming (nonparametric approach).

Data envelopment analysis (DEA) is the most frequently applied nonparametric methodology for estimating efficiency levels in the port industry. Charnes, Cooper, and Rhodes (1978) introduced the concept; Roll and Hayuth (1993) were the first to advocate its use in estimating efficiency in the port sector. Since then many researchers have used DEA to estimate port or terminal efficiency (see table A.1 for a list of DEA applications to container ports).

DEA is a deterministic nonparametric approach used to build a benchmark, the best practice frontier, based on available information. One of the main advantages of this approach is that computations are based exclusively on measures of physical outputs and inputs; prices, which are difficult to collect and compare, particularly at the international level, are not needed. Another advantage is that it takes into account the multi-output and multi-input dimensionality of production, a characteristic of the production function of ports. The calculations in this report assume that ports have as a production target the maximization of outputs for a given input combination. It therefore uses an output-oriented framework.

Two frontiers can be estimated, one assuming constant returns to scale and another assuming variable returns to scale. Scale efficiencies are computed and returns-to-scale (increasing, constant, or decreasing) identified for each port.[7]

The points A, B, C, D, and E in figure 2.5 illustrate the observed quantities of input used and output produced by different container ports. A is the only point at which a port is efficient under both constant and variable returns to scale. B and C are efficient under variable returns to scale, with B in the region of increasing returns to scale and C in the region of decreasing returns to scale. D and E are inefficient. They could produce more output with the same input quantity. Port E uses quantity $R$ of input $x$ to produce quantity $RE$ of output $y$.

**Figure 2.5  Constant and Variable Returns to Scale Frontiers in Data Envelopment Analysis**

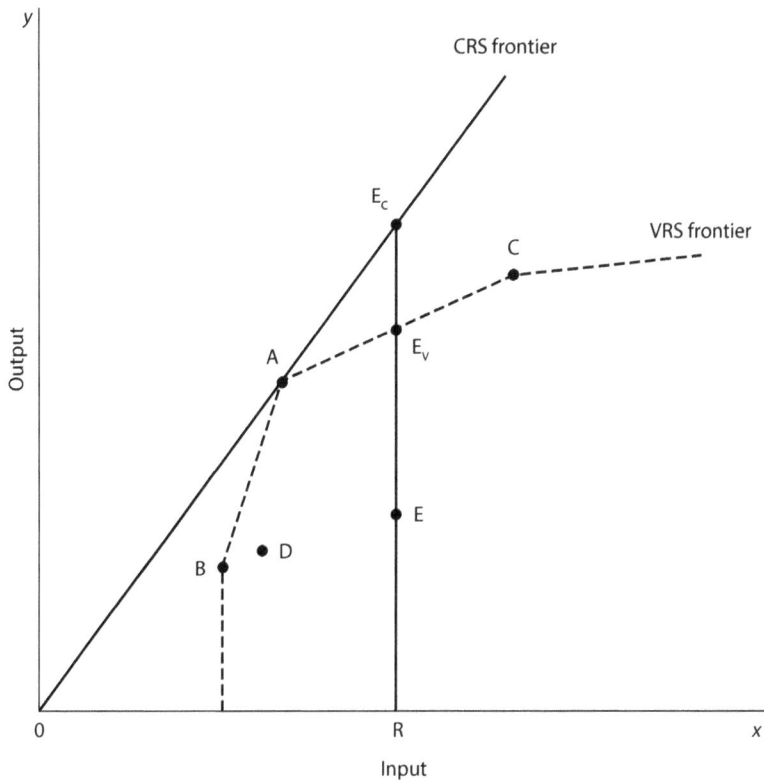

Source: Adapted from Färe and others 1994.
Note: CRS = constant returns to scale; VRS = variable returns to scale.

The vector $EE_C$ measures the distance to the best practice frontier. It can be decomposed into two parts. $EE_V$ corresponds to pure inefficiency; $E_VE_C$ denotes inefficiency caused by the scale of operation (scale inefficiency). Ports A and C form the piecewise linear combination benchmark with which port E is compared. The peers for port D are B and A. Under constant returns to scale, port A is the benchmark for all the other ports.

### Productivity Changes

Productivity is defined as the ratio of outputs to inputs. In a one-output one-input setting, computation of a productivity indicator is straightforward. In multi-output multi-input settings, the ratio needs to reflect an output factor over an input factor, known as total factor productivity (TFP). Various sources can account for variations in TFP across ports; partial productivity indicators may not be the most suitable tools with which to assess performance.

This report uses a Malmquist quantity index of TFP changes based on the nonparametric DEA approach (Färe and others 1994). Various methodologies were developed over the past several decades to estimate TFP changes. They are based on market prices (for example, price-based index numbers) or the estimation of production frontiers (for example, DEA or stochastic frontier analysis methods).[8] Approaches based on market prices do not allow for the decomposition of TFP changes into components, which estimation of production frontiers does.

Using the Malmquist quantity index allows TFP changes to be decomposed into a measure of technical progress (TC) of the activity level taken as a whole and a measure of efficiency change (EC):[9]

$$TFPC_M = TC \times \overbrace{PEC \times SEC}^{EC} \qquad (2.1)$$

EC can be further decomposed into two measures: pure efficiency change (PEC) and scale efficiency change (SEC). The measure of technical progress captures the shift of the best practice frontier; the measure of efficiency change captures how each port is catching up to the best practice frontier. Box 2.1 discusses the calculation of the Malmquist quantity index of TFP change, which it illustrates graphically.

The body of literature estimating the Malmquist index of TFP change has grown quickly over the past two decades (see table A.2). Färe and others (1994) first implemented the Malmquist productivity measure developed by Caves, Christensen, and Diewert (1982) in the context of efficiency theory. Since then this methodology has been applied in a wide range of industries, with the port sector receiving particular attention over the past decade.[10]

The proper choice of inputs and outputs is vital for DEA frontiers and Malmquist decomposition to provide meaningful results. Most studies include a bundle of variables representing labor and capital inputs. The inputs usually selected in the port literature are physical facilities (such as the number or size of berths, the number of gantry cranes, and equipment or terminal yardage) and labor force measures (Cullinane, Ji, and Wang 2005). The real monetary value of net assets in ports could also be considered, as Chang (1978) points out. Because of its potential sensitivity, this type of data is rarely available, however. On the output side, the number of container movements across the quayside is the usual choice for container ports (Cullinane and Song 2006; Cullinane and others 2005; Turner, Windle, and Dresner 2004).[11]

The facilities examined in this report follow the traditional approach. Capital is represented by total port area and the length of all container and multipurpose berths at the port. Labor inputs are derived from a predetermined relationship to cranes (direct data are not available). Following the approach used in the port literature (Cullinane, Ji, and Wang 2005; Cullinane and Wang 2010; Notteboom, Coeck, and van den Broeck 2000), the analysis includes the number of ship-to-shore or gantry cranes and the number of mobile or quay cranes with capacity of more than 15 tons as a proxy.[12] The number of twenty-foot equivalent units (TEUs) is used to measure output.

## Box 2.1  The Malmquist Index of Total Factor Productivity Change

In the simple one-output ($y$) one-input ($x$) setting depicted in figure B2.1.1, points $P_t$ and $P_{t+1}$ correspond to consecutive observations of port P in periods $t$ and $t + 1$, respectively. Based on available information for the sector, two DEA frontiers are computed, one for period $t$ and one for period $t + 1$, under the assumption of constant returns to scale. The efficiency of port P in period $t$ corresponds to the ratio $AP_t/AB$. In period $t + 1$, the efficiency of port P is given by the ratio $DP_{t+1}/DF$. Proceeding in the same way, and using the same information, it is possible to compute two auxiliary distance functions. One, given by $AP_t/AC$, measures the distance separating $P_t$ from the frontier in period $t + 1$ The other, given by $DP_{t+1}/DE$, measures the distance separating $P_{t+1}$ from the frontier computed in period $t$.

Following Färe and others (1994), the TFP change of port P from period $t$ to period $t + 1$ is computed as follows:

$$TFPC_M = \frac{TFP_{t+1}}{TFP_t} = \left( \frac{DP_{t+1}}{DE} \Big/ \frac{AP_t}{AB} \times \frac{DP_{t+1}}{DF} \Big/ \frac{AP_t}{AC} \right)^{0.5} \qquad (2.1.1)$$

### Figure B2.1.1  Malmquist Index of Total Factor Productivity Change

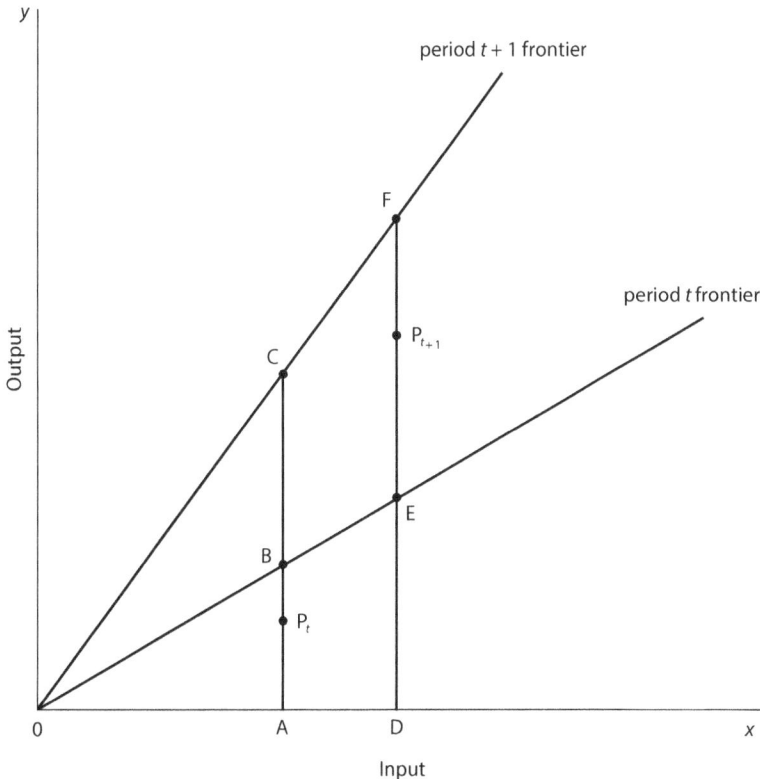

*Source:* Adapted from Färe and others 1994.

*box continues next page*

**Box 2.1  The Malmquist Index of Total Factor Productivity Change** (*continued*)

This formula can be restated as follows:

$$TFPC_M = \left( \frac{AC}{AB} \Big/ \frac{DF}{DE} \right)^{0.5} \times \left( \frac{DP_{t+1}}{DF} \Big/ \frac{AP_t}{AB} \right) \qquad (2.1.2)$$

The first term in parentheses on the right side of equation 2.1.2 captures technical change (TC). It corresponds to the frontier shift between period $t$ and $t + 1$ and is computed as the geometric mean of the change in technology between the two periods. The second term shows the productivity improvement of unit P between period $t$ and period $t + 1$ caused by efficiency change (EC). The sources of efficiency change can be identified through a further decomposition. As illustrated in figure 2.5, efficiency can be decomposed into pure efficiency and scale efficiency using constant and variable returns to scale frontiers. Adding variable returns to scale frontiers for period $t$ and $t + 1$ into figure B2.1.1 allows the second term in parentheses in equation 2.1.2 to be broken into pure efficiency and scale efficiency changes.

---

## Interregional Productivity Benchmarking

This subsection examines the evolution of container port productivity in South Asia relative to competing regions. In a globalized world in which technology and know-how can be easily acquired and the constant search for the most efficient supply chain drives international container flows, the performance of South Asian ports relative to that of competing ports becomes central. Competing ports were selected based on analysis of maritime routes through South Asia. Table 2.3 lists the ports included, by region.

The data were collected from various issues of the *Containerisation International Yearbook* for the period 2000–10. These reports do not cover all container ports in South Asia. The data in this report cover 14 of 20 South Asian container ports, which represent 98 percent of container traffic in the region.

East Asia has the largest number of ports in the sample, followed by South Asia (table 2.4). The standard deviations show significant dispersion in all regions. On average South Asian ports had a total throughput of about 750,000 TEUs during the period of analysis, with terminal areas averaging about 300,000 square meters and berth lengths about 1,000 meters. The average number of mobile cranes was about three, and the average number of ship-to-shore gantry cranes was about six.

On average, South Asian container ports experienced the most improvement in productivity between 2000 and 2010, with TFP increasing almost 80 percent (much more than the 55 percent increase in East Asia). Average TFP at containers ports in the Middle East and Southern and East Africa declined over this period. South Asia and East Asia moved closer to the frontier, leaving behind the Middle East and Southern and East Africa. Changes in TFP were driven largely by efficiency changes, not technical change (figure 2.6). There was no significant change in the production frontier of the industry between 2000 and 2010: The estimated technical

**Table 2.3 Container Ports Included in the Analysis**

| Region/country | Ports |
| --- | --- |
| **East Asia** | |
| China | Dalian, Guangzhou, Qingdao, Shanghai, Tianjin, Xiamen |
| Guam | Apra |
| Hong Kong SAR, China | Hong Kong |
| Malaysia | Kuantan, Kuching, Port Klang, Tanjung Pelepas, Tanjung Perak, Tanjung Priok |
| Philippines | Davao, Ilolio, Maila, Zamboanga |
| Singapore | Singapore |
| Taiwan, China | Kaoshiung, Keelung |
| Thailand | Bangkok, Laem Chabang |
| Vietnam | Danang, Haiphong, Ho Chi Minh |
| **Middle East** | |
| Jordan | Aqaba |
| Oman | Salalah |
| Saudi Arabia | Dammam, Jeddah, Jubail |
| United Arab Emirates | Dubai |
| Yemen, Rep. | Aden |
| **South Asia** | |
| Bangladesh | Chittagong |
| India | Chennai, Cochin, Jawaharlal Nehru (JNPT), Kandla, Kolkata, Mumbai, Mundra, Pipavav, Tuticorin, Visakhapatnam |
| Pakistan | Karachi, Port Qasim |
| Sri Lanka | Colombo |
| **Southern and East Africa** | |
| Kenya | Mombasa |
| Mauritius | Port Louis |
| South Africa | Cape Town, Durban, East London, Port Elizabeth |
| Sudan | Port Sudan |
| Tanzania | Dar es Salaam |

change index is near zero or even negative. This result reflects a catching-up process.

Further disaggregation of productivity changes indicates that both pure and scale efficiency were important (figure 2.7). In East Asia the efficiency changes that drove the increase in TFP primarily reflected better use of their facilities in handling containers (that is, catching-up with the variable returns to scale frontier). More efficient selection of the size of port facilities relative to output (that is, scale efficiency or catching-up with the constant returns to scale frontier) played a smaller role in East Asia. In South Asia both adjustment in the scale of facilities relative to throughput and better use of facilities helped increase TFP, with scale adjustment playing a marginally more important role. Both the scale of operation and the more efficient use of facilities also played important roles in Southern and East Africa and the Middle East.

**Table 2.4  Descriptive Port Statistics, by Region, 2000–10**

| Region | Number of ports | Statistic | Annual throughput (thousands of 20-foot equivalent units) | Terminal area (thousands of square meters) | Berth length (meters) | Number of mobile cranes | Number of ship-to-shore gantry cranes |
|---|---|---|---|---|---|---|---|
| East Asia | 26 | Average | 4,237 | 1,340 | 3,301 | 8.9 | 21.1 |
| | | Standard deviation | 6,299 | 1,662 | 3,014 | 23.5 | 28.3 |
| | | Maximum | 29,100 | 10,100 | 16,000 | 190 | 126 |
| | | Minimum | 26 | 15 | 100 | 0 | 0 |
| Middle East | 7 | Average | 1,798 | 1,066 | 1,729 | 4.3 | 14.4 |
| | | Standard deviation | 2,588 | 1,289 | 1,776 | 4.1 | 13.9 |
| | | Maximum | 11,800 | 8,092 | 13,460 | 22 | 78 |
| | | Minimum | 1 | 107 | 213 | 0 | 0 |
| South Asia | 14 | Average | 750 | 285 | 1,038 | 2.9 | 5.7 |
| | | Standard deviation | 953 | 287 | 785 | 5.9 | 7.5 |
| | | Maximum | 4,752 | 2,140 | 3,749 | 23 | 26 |
| | | Minimum | 18 | 3 | 168 | 0 | 0 |
| Southern and East Africa | 8 | Average | 547 | 496 | 1,148 | 1.5 | 6 |
| | | Standard deviation | 612 | 506 | 795 | 4.3 | 6.2 |
| | | Maximum | 2,643 | 1,940 | 2,854 | 17 | 25 |
| | | Minimum | 26 | 22 | 278 | 0 | 0 |

*Source:* Data from *Containerisation International Yearbook* 2002–12.

**Figure 2.6  Average Changes in and Drivers of Total Factor Productivity at Ports between 2000 and 2010, by Region**

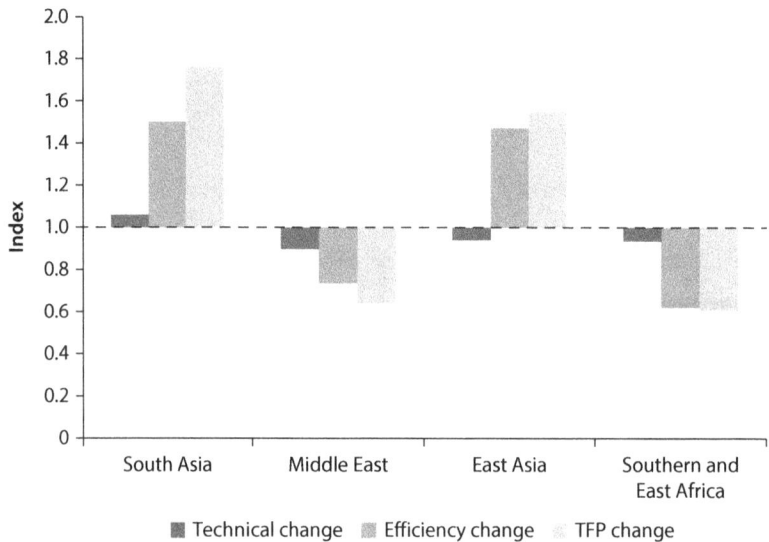

**Figure 2.7 Importance of Scale and Pure Efficiency Effects in Changes of Port Efficiency between 2000 and 2010, by Region**

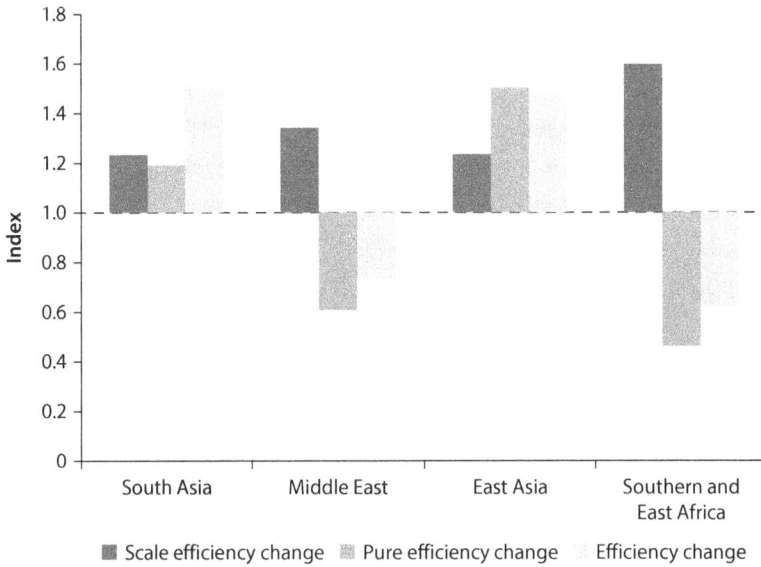

Scale efficiency change ▪ Pure efficiency change ▪ Efficiency change

## Interregional Efficiency Benchmarking

This section assesses the evolution of efficiency. A single production frontier was calculated using throughput and facilities for the 2000–10 period for the same 55 container ports used in the TFP analysis. Figure 2.8 presents the average pure efficiency for each region.[13] The low levels of average efficiency indicate that most container ports performed at low levels of efficiency.

Average pure efficiency rose in all regions. Improvement was greatest in South Asia, which reduced the gap with East Asia. In the first half of the decade, average pure efficiency decreased more in South Asia than in East Asia; South Asia improved by more in the second half of the decade. South Asia also experienced the strongest rebound after the 2009 crisis. Efficiency gains in South Asia are improving its international competitiveness.

At the end of the decade, South Asia seemed to be better positioned than East Asia to increase the efficiency of its container ports through scale expansions. All four regions present significant scale inefficiencies, with at least three-quarters of container ports showing either increasing or decreasing returns to scale between 2008 and 2010.

Table 2.5 contrasts ports in East Asia and South Asia. Scale inefficiency in East Asia is concentrated mainly in the decreasing returns to scale part of the production function, a reflection of the expansion in capacity during the 2000s and the contraction in trade at the end of the decade as a result of the economic crisis. In South Asia scale inefficiency is concentrated in the increasing returns to scale part of the production function.

The results of returns to scale diagnosis correspond with intuition. On average, ports in South Asia, the Middle East, and Southern and East Africa are smaller

**Figure 2.8  Average Pure Efficiency Scores, by Region, 2000–10**

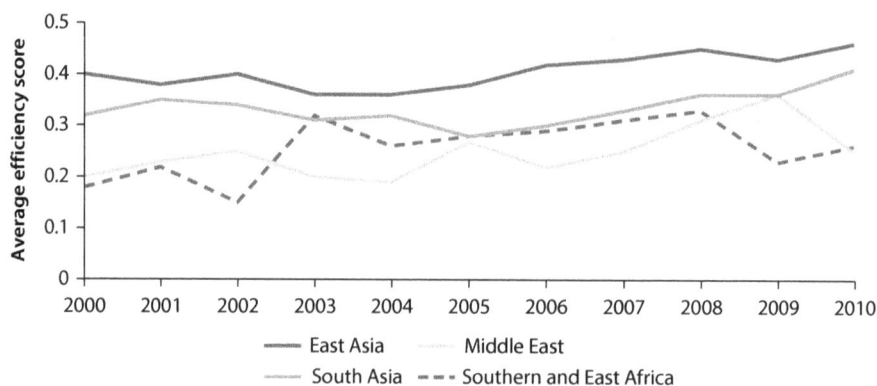

*Note:* Efficiency scores were estimated using intertemporal data envelopment analysis assuming variable returns to scale.

**Table 2.5  Returns to Scale Shares of Container Ports, by Region, 2008–10**

| Region | Increasing returns to scale | Constant returns to scale | Decreasing returns to scale |
|---|---|---|---|
| East Asia | 30 | 17 | 53 |
| Middle East | 60 | 16 | 24 |
| South Asia | 62 | 24 | 14 |
| Southern and East Africa | 75 | 25 | 0 |

than those in East Asia. Given that the production technology of ports is characterized by large fixed investments, it is logical to expect that smaller ports are still in the increasing returns to scale zone of the production function.

The relevant policy question is whether ports can influence the scale of operations. The answer depends on many factors, including the availability of land on which to build new facilities, the capacity of hinterland connectivity, the existence of competition, the congestion of existing facilities, and the nature of traffic (transshipment or domestic). Ports are limited in their ability to affect demand. Like most transport infrastructure, they face derived demand and consequently cannot significantly alter outputs when they change inputs. Salient exceptions are ports that suffer strong congestion or transshipment ports that are vertically integrated (formally or through agreements) with shipping lines, but these exceptions are valid only for port expansion (increase in inputs). When ports face output contraction caused by factors completely out of their control, such as a global economic crisis, there is little they can do to adjust the scale of operation, as inputs remain constant when output falls.

### Benchmarking Port Efficiency in South Asia

This section analyzes the evolution of efficiency of container ports in South Asia. It is based on pure and scale efficiency scores for 14 container ports, estimated based on DEA production frontiers built using only those ports. The reason for limiting the analysis to South Asia frontiers is to ensure that the changes observed at the port level are not driven by the behavior of ports outside the region. The computation of the frontier relies on the same inputs and output used in the analysis presented above.

Table 2.6 presents the results from a DEA efficiency analysis assuming variable returns to scale in which a single production frontier for 2000–10 is computed in order to benchmark ports against one another.[14] Each row shows the efficiency evolution from 2000 to 2010.[15] The scores, which range from 0 (most inefficient) to 1 (most efficient), represent pure efficiency.

Average pure efficiency in South Asia increased between 2000 and 2010, rising from 0.50 to 0.64 (average pure efficiency of 0.64 means that on average the South Asian ports in the sample could increase their throughput by more than half with the facilities they currently use).[16] Average pure efficiency declined between 2000 and 2003, partly because of the impact of two new container ports, Pipavav and Mundra, which started commercial operation of their container terminals in 2002 and 2003, respectively. Initial investments in both ports caused their ratios to be low in the first few years.[17] Excluding these ports, average pure efficiency rose from 0.50 to 0.67 between 2000 and 2010.

The increase in average pure efficiency hides important differences across ports. At the beginning of the decade, Mumbai and Tuticorin were the most efficient container ports in the region. Their positions dropped later in the decade. In contrast, the pure efficiency scores of Chittagong, Colombo, JNPT, Mundra, Qasim, and Kolkata improved remarkably over the decade.[18] At the beginning of the decade, Kolkata performed poorly, with an efficiency score of 0.24; at the end of the decade, its efficiency score hovered around 1.0.

**Table 2.6 Pure Efficiency Scores of South Asian Container Ports, 2000–10**

| Port | 2000 | 2001 | 2002 | 2003 | 2004 | 2005 | 2006 | 2007 | 2008 | 2009 | 2010 |
|---|---|---|---|---|---|---|---|---|---|---|---|
| Chennai | 0.41 | 0.40 | 0.45 | 0.43 | 0.42 | 0.49 | 0.64 | 0.71 | 0.81 | 0.82 | 1.00 |
| Chittagong | 0.34 | 0.37 | 0.42 | 0.47 | 0.52 | 0.59 | 0.66 | 0.72 | 0.81 | 0.87 | 1.00 |
| Cochin | 0.24 | 0.28 | 0.30 | 0.31 | 0.23 | 0.25 | 0.28 | 0.30 | 0.32 | 0.36 | 0.46 |
| Colombo | 0.85 | 0.85 | 0.53 | 0.53 | 0.60 | 0.67 | 0.84 | 0.92 | 1.00 | 0.87 | 1.00 |
| JNPT | 0.56 | 0.74 | 0.90 | 0.82 | 0.86 | 0.96 | 0.81 | 1.00 | 0.97 | 0.38 | 1.00 |
| Kandla | 0.57 | 0.70 | 0.87 | 0.94 | 1.00 | 0.56 | 0.41 | 0.38 | 0.32 | 0.19 | 0.30 |
| Karachi | 0.31 | 0.85 | 0.88 | 0.49 | 0.51 | 0.63 | 0.31 | 0.58 | 0.60 | 0.62 | 0.54 |
| Kolkata | 0.24 | 0.39 | 0.46 | 0.49 | 0.34 | 0.63 | 0.70 | 0.85 | 0.86 | 1.00 | 0.92 |
| Mumbai | 1.00 | 0.79 | 0.66 | 0.61 | 0.68 | 0.49 | 0.43 | 0.37 | 0.29 | 0.18 | 0.23 |
| Mundra | — | — | — | 0.05 | 0.58 | 0.27 | 0.44 | 0.33 | 0.41 | 0.42 | 0.56 |
| Pipavav | — | — | 0.03 | 0.03 | 0.07 | 0.10 | 0.10 | 0.08 | 0.14 | 0.26 | 0.38 |
| Qasim | 0.34 | 0.35 | 0.48 | 0.35 | 0.52 | 0.60 | 0.74 | 0.79 | 0.76 | 0.83 | 0.86 |
| Tuticorin | 1.00 | 0.44 | 0.44 | 0.54 | 0.33 | 0.35 | 0.41 | 0.49 | 0.47 | 0.47 | 0.50 |
| Visakhapatnam | 0.07 | 0.07 | 0.07 | 0.03 | 0.07 | 0.07 | 0.08 | 0.10 | 0.13 | 0.15 | 0.19 |
| Average | 0.50 | 0.52 | 0.50 | 0.44 | 0.48 | 0.47 | 0.49 | 0.54 | 0.56 | 0.53 | 0.64 |

*Note:* Efficiency scores were estimated using an intertemporal data envelopment analysis assuming variable returns to scale. 0 = most inefficient; 1 = most efficient; — = not available.

Kolkata experienced a remarkable increase from 2004 onward, when ABG Kolkata Container Terminal Pvt. Ltd. started operating and the port experienced a significant increase in traffic.[19] Improvement at Chittagong can also be explained by a significant increase in port traffic; port facilities there increased marginally at best. Both Kolkata and Chittagong had to meet growing demand without significant expansion of capacity, which they did by increasing efficiency in the use of port facilities. However, as the results of the operational performance analysis show, Kolkata (including Haldia Docks) and Chittagong are the ports at which container vessels spent the longest time at berth throughout the decade, with little improvement (see table 2.1). The percentage of idle time at berth is also high, particularly at Kolkata. Colombo increased the efficiency in the use of its facilities and improved its operational performance by almost halving the share of idle time at berth.

JNPT is a success story: The introduction of private competition at the end of the last century triggered progressive improvement in efficiency. Traffic rose sharply when the Nhava Sheva International Container Terminal (operated by DP World) came on line in July 2000, easing congestion at the existing terminal, where utilization levels had gone beyond suitable levels of 70 percent of capacity.[20] The economic crisis at the end of the decade hurt JNPT, as throughput dropped significantly. Expansion of JNPT and improvement in efficiency in the use of its facilities reduced Mumbai's efficiency scores, which declined as shippers switched to JNPT.

The emergence of Mundra and Pipavav introduced competition between ports on the west cost of India. Mundra, one of the early nonmajor ports, developed through significant private sector involvement. Its rise led to the divergence of container cargo from JNPT, especially for cargo destined for or originating from the northern hinterland of India (Delhi, Punjab, Haryana, North Rajasthan, and Uttarakhand). Significantly more traffic was diverted to Mundra than to Pipavav. The difference reflected Pipavav's limited tie-ups with shipping lines and its lack of sufficient container handling infrastructure (container freight stations) outside the port to cater to road-based cargo from Gujarat and South Rajasthan. In the case of Mundra, APSEZ, its parent company, also operates container trains and inland container depots through its logistics subsidiary, allowing it to provide a more integrated logistics service.

The Port of Kandla attempted to respond to competition without success. The share of Gujarat ports, especially Mundra, in the traffic of the northwestern corridor has risen steadily since Mundra was commissioned. Mundra has grew steadily at almost 35 percent a year. Its growth particularly hurt Kandla, which was not able to attract large vessels, because of its relatively shallow draft. Kandla gradually reduced its total throughput after 2004, even though it expanded its capacity to handle containers. As a consequence, its pure efficiency dropped to 0.30 by 2010.

The pure efficiency of South Asian container ports converged between 2003 and 2010. A contemporaneous efficiency analysis that compares ports against one another during a single year was undertaken for 2003 and 2010.[21]

That analysis shows that the standard deviation of contemporaneous efficiency scores decreased, from 0.37 in 2003 to 0.30 in 2010 (figure 2.9).

The average scale efficiency of South Asian container ports declined slightly over the decade, falling from 0.94 to 0.89. The inefficiency was concentrated in the increasing returns to scale area of the production function. Of the eight ports that were on the variable returns to scale frontier for some years, Colombo, JNPT, and Kolkata were the only ports that were not on the constant returns to scale frontier the same years.[22] This result means that they were efficient in the use of their facilities but not with respect to the size of their facilities relative to their throughput during those years.

### Benchmarking Interregional Port Efficiency

This section examines how each South Asian container port compares with other ports in the Indian and Western Pacific Oceans in the use of their facilities. The analysis is based on data from 2010.

Ports were divided into three groups, based on annual throughput: large (more than 4 million TEUs), medium-size (0.5–4 million TEUs), and small (less than 0.5 million TEUs). Ports in each category were further classified into three groups: top performers (efficiency score of 1), above-average performers (efficiency scores above the average for their category but below 1), and below-average performers (efficiency scores below the average for their category) (table 2.7).

Large and medium-size container ports tend to be clustered at the bottom and small ports at the top in 2010. East Asian ports dominated the large-port group. All Chinese ports in the sample were in this group. In contrast, most Indian ports were in the small and medium-size categories. The average efficiency scores in 2010 were 0.61 for large, 0.56 for medium-size, and 0.81 for small ports. These figures reflect the fact that 50 percent of small ports but just 20 percent of large ports and 12 percent of medium-size ports ranked as top performers.

**Figure 2.9 Standard Deviation of Pure Efficiency Scores at Container Ports in South Asia, 2003–10**

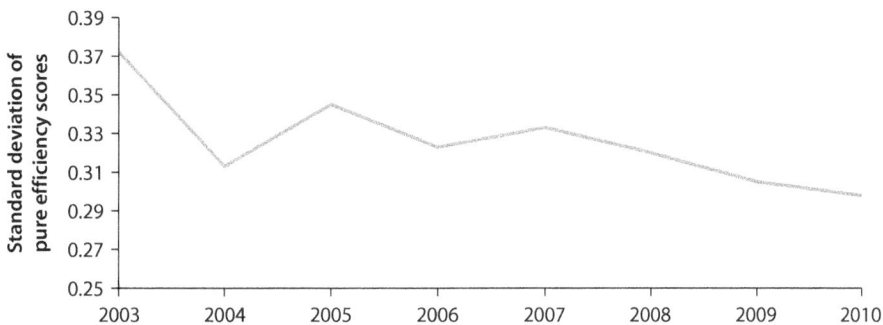

*Note:* Pure efficiency scores were computed using one frontier per year (contemporaneous frontier).

**Table 2.7  Pure Efficiency of Selected Container Ports, by Size, 2010**

| Port size | Large (more than 4 million TEUs) | Medium (0.5–4 million TEUs) | Small (less than 0.5 million TEUs) |
|---|---|---|---|
| Average pure efficiency | 0.61 | 0.56 | 0.81 |
| Top performers | Shanghai (China), Singapore (Singapore), Xiamen (China) | Chittagong (Bangladesh), Davao (Philippines) | Cochin (India), Dar es Salaam (Tanzania), Iloilo (Philippines), Kimbe (Papua New Guinea), Kuantan (Malaysia), Kuching (Malaysia), Mumbai (India), Pipavav (India), Port Louis (Mauritius), Port Sudan (Sudan), Tuticorin (India) |
| Above-average performers | Dubai (UAE), Guangzhou (China), Kaohsiung (Taiwan, China), Qingdao (China), Tianjin (China) | Durban (South Africa), Jedda (Saudi Arabia), Keelung (Taiwan, China), Kolkata (India), Salalah (Oman), Tanjung Perak (Indonesia) | Aden (Yemen, Rep.), Ho Chi Minh (Vietnam), Jubail (Saudi Arabia), Kandla (India) |
| Below-average performers | Colombo (Sri Lanka), Dalian (China), JNPT (India), Laem Chabang (Thailand), Port Klang (Malaysia), Tanjung Pelepas (Malaysia), Tanjung Priok (Malaysia) | Aqaba (Jordan), Bangkok (Thailand), Cape Town (South Africa), Chennai (India), Haiphong (Vietnam), Karachi (Pakistan), Mundra (India), Mombasa (Kenya), Qasim (Pakistan) | Apra (Guam), Danang (Vietnam), East London (South Africa), Manila (Philippines), Port Elizabeth (South Africa), Visakhapatnam (India), Zamboanga (Philippines) |

*Note:* Ports in each category are listed in alphabetical order, not order of performance.

JNPT and Colombo are the top performers in South Asia, but they fare poorly compared with similar container ports in the Indian and Western Pacific Oceans. The pure efficiency of South Asian container ports relative to their peers in the Indian and Western Pacific Oceans is inversely correlated with size. Large ports, such as JNPT and Colombo, have below-average efficiency scores for their category, a concern because of the significant proportion of regional traffic they handle. If Colombo wants to become the next Singapore—the main transshipment port on the maritime route between Asia and Europe and the United States—it needs to improve the use of its facilities. Medium-size container ports fare better in the interregional comparison, but half of them are below-average performers for their size group. By contrast, two-thirds of small South Asian container ports rank among the top performers in their size group, with only Visakhapatnam below average.

## Concluding Remarks

Container traffic in South Asia increased by a factor of more than four between 2000 and 2012. Although the efficiency of use of time at berths rose during the period, South Asian container ports lost their operational edge relative to ports in other regions between 2006 and 2011, as other regions significantly reduced the time needed to turn around container vessels. The more efficient use of time at the berthing stage and improvements in the scale of operations were the main drivers of changes in TFP in South Asia.

South Asia caught up with East Asia between 2000 and 2010 in terms of efficiency in the use of container port facilities. South Asian container ports experienced the most improvement in average TFP among ports in the Indian and Western Pacific Oceans (80 percent versus 55 percent for East Asia) between 2000 and 2010. The scale of ports in South Asia improved, although significant potential to improve overall efficiency through scale expansion exists, as indicated by the fact that 62 percent of South Asian container ports enjoyed increasing returns to scale between 2008 and 2010. East Asia had more slack capacity toward the end of the 2000s (53 percent of ports had decreasing returns to scale), in large part because of the slowdown in trade in the region and the large investments in the last two decades.

South Asian container ports have the potential to handle significantly more traffic than they currently do. The benchmarking of container ports in the Indian and Western Pacific Oceans shows that in 2010 the sector had room to more than double its throughput with existing facilities. One could argue that adopting and mastering technology takes time and that other regions, such as East Asia, are performing better because they had a head start, that South Asian ports are doing well for their level of development. However, even if this argument were true, a benchmarking that considers only South Asian ports indicates that in 2010 the container port sector in the region had room to increase its average throughput by more than 50 percent with existing facilities.

Some ports, such as Mundra, JNPT, Qasim, and Colombo, experienced significant improvements in the use of container port facilities between 2000 and 2010. Others, such as Mumbai and Tuticorin, moved in the opposite direction. Colombo, which improved its operational performance by almost halving the share of idle time at berth, ranked as one of the top South Asian ports in 2010 in terms of operational and economic performance. Chittagong and Kolkata, which ranked well in terms of the use of their facilities in 2010, ranked poorly on operational performance, with the two longest vessel turnaround times in the region.

## Notes

1. For research on the combination of benchmarking and regulation, see Agrell and Bogetoft (2010, 2011, 2013) and Coelli and others (2003).

2. For a survey of the empirical literature on efficiency and productivity in the port sector, see González and Trujillo (2008) and Suárez-Alemán and others (2016).

3. Data for South Asian ports are annual averages; Ducruet, Itoh, and Merk (2014) data, which are for May, may capture some seasonal effects.

4. The economic literature also considers a third component of efficiency: allocative efficiency, the mix of inputs that minimizes production costs for a given level of outputs given input prices. Changes in allocative efficiency do not have direct effects on

productivity. The analysis in this section does not address allocative efficiency, because prices are very difficult to collect and compare, particularly at the international level.

5. Improvements in scale efficiency are possible in a productive environment with increasing or decreasing returns to scale. In a constant return to scale environment, productivity will not change.

6. Nonexpert readers interested in efficiency estimation are encouraged to read *A Primer on Efficiency Measurement for Utilities and Transport Regulators*, by Coelli and others (2003).

7. Constant returns to scale means that when all production inputs are doubled, output also doubles. Increasing (decreasing) returns to scale means that when all production inputs are doubled, output more (less) than doubles.

8. Coelli and others (2003) provided a detailed review of these methodologies.

9. An advantage of this index is that prices are not needed in order to calculate it. Its main disadvantage compared with traditional index numbers is that it cannot be computed separately for each unit. Its computation relies on the estimation of sequential frontiers. Panel data must be available for representative units operating in the sector.

10. Other sectors analyzed include banking (see Guzman and Reverte 2008; Matthews and Zhang 2010; Portela and Thanassoulis 2006); agriculture (see Brümmer, Glauben, and Lu 2002; Tauer 1998; Umetsu, Lekprichakul, and Chakravorty 2003); the environment (see Kortelainen 2008; Kumar 2006; Zhou, Ang, and Han 2010); and sanitation (see Färe and others 1994; Ganon 2008; Kontodimopoulos and Niakas 2006).

11. There is consensus on the multi-output nature of more general port activity; there is no agreement on the measurement of outputs in terms of either the physical quantity of merchandise or the revenue derived from it (González and Trujillo 2008). Recent papers that address general ports, such as Barros (2003), consider a larger number of outputs, such as the number of ship calls, the movement of freight, market share, different types of cargo, and net profit, among others. Coto-Millán, Baños Pino, and Rodríguez Álvarez (2000), for example, incorporate cargo moved, boarded and unboarded passengers, and vehicles with passengers as outputs.

12. The analysis in the report follows the assumption made in Serebrisky and others (2016) for the Latin American case, which considers only the cranes that are able to manage containers, in order avoid overestimating container terminal facilities.

13. Average pure efficiency for the Middle East and Southern and East Africa varied more, mainly because of the smaller number of ports from those regions in the sample.

14. The literature on production frontiers calls this approach of estimating a single frontier using observations for several years the intertemporal approach. An alternative is to follow a contemporaneous approach and calculate one frontier for each year. Such an approach allows ports to be compared against one another only in a single year.

15. Results from DEA assuming constant returns to scale are highly correlated to the results from DEA assuming variable returns to scale (0.98). Although each DEA specification reports different outcomes (as they take into account different frameworks and assumptions), both analyses show a moderate increase in overall efficiency over the decade.

16. The results from the intraregional analysis are not in conflict with the results from the interregional analysis in previous section; estimations made using different assumptions about returns to scale and different samples of ports produce different frontiers.

17. The pure efficiency score for Karachi also dropped significantly between 2002 and 2003, as a result of a 40 percent decrease in throughput.

18. Chittagong's efficiency scores may be overestimated, as almost half of container traffic is handled at general cargo berths through geared ships, an operational pattern that the data on facilities do not capture. Possible overestimation would not affect the trend of efficiency scores, however. Chittagong has not increased its facilities in several years, but the container throughput it handles has continuously increased at about 10 percent a year.

19. In 2004 ABG Kolkata Container Terminal Pvt. Ltd. was awarded the contract to supply, operate, and maintain the equipment for handling containers at the Port of Kolkata.

20. Two of the three terminals at JNPT, India's largest container port, were developed and are operated by private players on a build-operate-transfer (BOT) concession from the Port Trust. The Port Trust operates the first terminal itself. DP World operates the second (the Nhava Sheva International Container Terminal). A joint venture between the largest container train operator in the country (Concor) and APM Terminals operates the third. PSA recently won the concession to operate the fourth terminal.

21. The years 2003 and 2010 were selected because the same number of ports operated between the two years.

22. Colombo was on the variable and constant returns to scale frontiers in 2008 but not 2010.

## References

Agrell, P. J., and P. Bogetoft. 2010. "Harmonizing the Nordic Regulation of Electricity Distribution." In *Energy, Natural Resources and Environmental Economics*, edited by E. Bjørndal, M. Bjørndal, P. M. Pardalos, and M. Rönnqvist, 293–316. Berlin: Springer.

———. 2011. *Development of Benchmarking Models for Distribution System Operators in Belgium*. Commission de Régulation de l'Éléctricité et du Gaz (CREG).

———. 2013. "Benchmarking and Regulation." *Benchmarking* 8: 1–33.

Barros, C. P. 2003. "The Measurement of Efficiency of Portuguese Sea Port Authorities with DEA." *International Journal of Transport Economics* 30 (3): 335–54.

Brümmer, B., T. Glauben, and W. Lu. 2006. "Policy Reform and Productivity Change in Chinese Agriculture: A Distance Function Approach." *Journal of Development Economics* 81 (1): 61–79.

Caves, D., L. Christensen, and W. E. Diewert. 1982. "The Economic Theory of Index Numbers and the Measurement of Input, Output, and Productivity." *Econometrica* 50: 73–86.

Centre on Regulation in Europe. 2011. "Regulating for Efficiency: Is Benchmarking Enough? Summary of Presentations and Discussions." CERRE Regulation Forum, Brussels.

Chang, S. 1978. "In Defence of Port Economic Impact Studies." *Transportation Journal* 17 (3): 79–85.

Charnes, A., W. W. Cooper, and E. Rhodes. 1978. "Measuring the Efficiency of Decision Making Units." *European Journal of Operational Research* 2 (6): 429–44.

Coelli, T. J., A. Estache, S. Perelman, and L. Trujillo. 2003. *A Primer on Efficiency Measurement for Utilities and Transport Regulators.* Washington, DC: World Bank.

Coelli, T. J., D. S. P. Rao, C. J. O'Donnell, and G. E. Battese. 2005. *An Introduction to Efficiency and Productivity Analysis.* New York: Springer.

Coto Millán, P., J. Baños Pino, and A. Rodríguez Álvarez. 2000. "Economic Efficiency in Spanish Ports: Some Empirical Evidence." *Maritime Policy and Management* 27 (2): 169–74.

Cullinane, K. P. B., P. Ji, and T. Wang. 2005. "The Relationship between Privatization and DEA Estimates of Efficiency in the Container Port Industry." *Journal of Economics and Business* 57 (5): 433–62.

Cullinane, K. P. B., and D. W. Song. 2006. "Estimating the Relative Efficiency of European Container Ports: A Stochastic Frontier Analysis." *Port Economics: Research in Transportation Economics* 16 (1): 85–115.

Cullinane, K. P. B., and T. Wang. 2010. "The Efficiency Analysis of Container Port Production Using DEA Panel Data Approaches." *OR Spectrum* 32 (3): 717–38.

Defilippi, E. 2010. *Access Regulation for Naturally Monopolistic Port Terminals: Lessons from Regulated Network Industries.* No. EPS-2010-204-LIS, Erasmus Research Institute of Management, Rotterdam.

Defilippi, E., and L. Flor. 2008. "Regulation in a Context of Limited Competition: A Port Case." *Transportation Research Part A: Policy and Practice* 42 (5): 762–73.

Ducruet, C., H. Itoh, and O. Merk. 2014. "Time Efficiency at World Container Ports." Discussion Paper 2014-08, International Transport Forum, OECD, Paris.

Estache, A., B. Tovar, and L. Trujillo. 2004. "Sources of Efficiency Gains in Port Reform: A DEA Decomposition of a Malmquist TFP Index for Mexico." *Utilities Policy* 12 (4): 221–30.

Färe, R., S. Grosskopf, M. Norris, and Z. Zhang. 1994. "Productivity Growth, Technical Progress, and Efficiency Change in Industrialized Countries." *American Economic Review* 84 (1): 66–83.

Gannon, B. 2008. "Total Factor Productivity Growth of Hospitals in Ireland: A Nonparametric Approach." *Applied Economics Letters* 15 (2): 131–35.

González, M., and L. Trujillo. 2008. "Reforms and Infrastructure Efficiency in Spain's Container Ports." *Transportation Research Part A* 42 (1): 243–57.

Guzman, I., and C. Reverte. 2008. "Productivity and Efficiency Change and Shareholder Value: Evidence from the Spanish Banking Sector." *Applied Economics* 40 (15): 2033–40.

Kontodimopoulos, N., and D. Niakas. 2006. "A 12-Year Analysis of Malmquist Total Factor Productivity in Dialysis Facilities." *Journal of Medical Systems* 30 (5): 333–42.

Kortelainen, M. 2008. "Dynamic Environmental Performance Analysis: A Malmquist Index Approach." *Ecological Economics* 64 (4): 701–15.

Kumar, S. 2006. "Environmentally Sensitive Productivity Growth: A Global Analysis Using Malmquist–Luenberger Index." *Ecological Economics* 56 (2): 280–93.

Lloyd's List. 2002–12. *Containerisation International Yearbook.* London.

Matthews, K., and N. X. Zhang. 2010. "Bank Productivity in China 1997–2007: Measurement and Convergence." *China Economic Review* 21 (4): 617–28.

Ministry of Road Transport and Highways. 2014. *Basic Port Statistics of India.* Transport Research Wing, Government of India, New Delhi.

Notteboom, T., C. Coeck, and J. van den Broeck. 2000. "Measuring and Explaining the Relative Efficiency of Container Terminals by Means of Bayesian Stochastic Frontier Models." *International Journal of Maritime Economics* 2 (2): 83–106.

Portela, M. C. A. S., and E. Thanassoulis. 2006. "Malmquist Indexes Using a Geometric Distance Function (GDF). Application to a Sample of Portuguese Bank Branches." *Journal of Productivity Analysis* 25 (1–2): 25–41.

Roll, Y., and Yehuda Hayuth. 1993. "Port Performance Comparison Applying Data Envelopment Analysis. DEA." *Maritime Policy and Management* 20 (2): 153–61.

Serebrisky, T. 2012. *Airport Economics in Latin America and the Caribbean: Benchmarking, Regulation, and Pricing.* Washington, DC: World Bank.

Serebrisky, T., J. Morales Sarriera, A. Suárez-Alemán, G. Araya, C. Briceño-Garmendía, and J. Schwartz. 2016. "Exploring the drivers of port efficiency in Latin America and the Caribbean." *Transport Policy* 45: 31–45.

Suárez-Alemán, A., J. Morales Sarriera, T. Serebrisky, and L. Trujillo. 2016. "When it comes to container port efficiency, are all developing regions equal?." *Transportation Research Part A: policy and practice* 86, 56–77.

Talley, W. K. 2012. "Ports in Theory." In *The Blackwell Companion to Maritime Economics*, edited by Wayne K. Talley, 473–90. Oxford: Wiley Blackwell.

Tauer, L. W. 1998. "Productivity of New York Dairy Farms Measured by Nonparametric Malmquist Indices." *Journal of Agricultural Economics* 49 (2): 234–49.

Tongzon, J. L. 1995. "Determinants of Port Performance and Efficiency." *Transportation Research Part A: Policy and Practice* 29 (3): 245–52.

Turner, H., R. Windle, and M. Dresner. 2004. "North American Container Port Productivity: 1984/1997." *Transportation Research Part E* 40 (4): 339–56.

Umetsu, C., T. Lekprichakul, and U. Chakravorty. 2003. "Efficiency and Technical Change in the Philippine Rice Sector: A Malmquist Total Factor Productivity Analysis." *American Journal of Agricultural Economics* 85 (4): 943–63.

UNCTAD (United Nations Conference on Trade and Development). 1976. "Port Performance Indicators." TD/B/C.4/131/Supp.1/Rev.1.

World Bank. 2007. *Port Reform Toolkit*, 2nd ed. Washington, DC: World Bank. http://www.ppiaf.org/sites/ppiaf.org/files/documents/toolkits/portoolkit/toolkit/index.html.

Zhou, P., B. W. Ang, and J. Y. Han. 2010. "Total Factor Carbon Emission Performance: A Malmquist Index Analysis." *Energy Economics* 32 (1): 194–201.

# CHAPTER 3

# Drivers of Container Port Performance in South Asia

## Introduction

The South Asian container port sector improved its average performance with respect to most indicators between 2000 and 2010, as chapter 2 shows. The improvement hides contrasting patterns across South Asian ports, however. Some ports experienced significant improvements during the decade, while others struggled to sustain their performance. The relevant policy question is how to turn the good examples into the norm across the region. Understanding the reasons behind dissimilar performance may provide answers.

Some factors that affect port performance—trade flows, custom regulations, the domestic transport network—are beyond the control of port authorities and shipping ministries. This chapter examines the most important factors over which they do have control. The first section looks at the relationship between private sector participation and port performance. The second section looks at the relationship between port governance characteristics and port performance. The third section looks at the relationship between port competition and port performance. The last section provides some concluding remarks.

## Does Private Sector Participation Improve Port Performance?

Port operations are governed and managed according to a number of different models, which vary according to the level of involvement of the public versus the private sector. The four main models are the public service, tool, landlord, and private port models (box 3.1 briefly presents the main characteristics of each model).

Globally, bringing the private sector into port operations has been a critical feature of port reform. The key objective for the government is to transfer responsibilities and risks to the private sector. The risk-transfer arrangement is organized via an agreement with a private sector entity that articulates the responsibilities, rights, and liabilities, including payments, of each. The degree of

---

**Box 3.1  Public Service, Tool, Landlord, and Private Models of Ports Explained**

Under the public service model, a port authority offers the complete range of services required for the functioning of the seaport system. It owns, maintains, and operates every asset (fixed and mobile). Cargo-handling activities are executed by workers employed directly by the port authority.

The tool port model is similar to the public service model. Under this model, the port authority owns, develops, and maintains the port infrastructure as well as the superstructure, including cargo-handling equipment, such as quay cranes and forklift trucks. Cargo handling on board vessels and on the apron and quay is usually carried out by private firms contracted by shipping agents or other principals licensed by the port authority. The tool port model has been often used as an intermediate step in transitioning from a service port to a landlord port.

Landlord ports are characterized by their mixed public-private orientation. Under this model, the port authority acts as regulatory body and landlord, and private companies operate the port. Infrastructure is leased to private operating companies. Private operators provide and maintain their own superstructure, own and operate the cargo-handling equipment, and in most cases employ the dock labor. The private operator pays a lease plus a revenue share (if any) to the landlord port authority in the case of a leasehold agreement. In the case of a concession agreement, the concessionaire pays the government for concession rights or the government pays the concessionaire for services it offers.

Very few ports operate under a private model. They are usually the result of the sale of port land and the transfer of regulatory functions to the private sector. Under this model, the private sector owns all port land and infrastructure. The state has no meaningful involvement or public policy interest in the port sector. The port owner has full flexibility and autonomy of owning and selling the assets (including land) for maritime or nonmaritime use. Private ports are essentially self-regulating entities with minimal or no regulatory oversight.

---

risk-sharing between the public and private sector varies across port models (figure 3.1). The landlord port model is now viewed as best practice for port ownership and management structure. In this model, a government, often through a port authority, enters into an agreement with private port operator(s).

The literature documents some positive role of private sector involvement in the efficiency of container terminals. Cullinane and Song (2003) assess the efficiency of container terminals in the Republic of Korea and the United Kingdom. They find support for the hypothesis that productive efficiency in the sector improved following the introduction of private participation and deregulation policies. Notteboom, Coeck, and van den Broeck (2000) reach a similar conclusion after comparing the efficiency levels of 36 European and 4 Asian containers ports. Cullinane, Song, and Gray (2002) find that the level of market deregulation has a positive influence on performance.

Different forms of private participation are associated with different outcomes. In a comparative study of port reforms in Australia and New Zealand, Tull and Reveley (2001) find that port reform fundamentally improved ports in both countries but with differential impact on various stakeholders. On the whole, the New Zealand port companies performed well for shareholders; they performed less well from the perspective of some port users, especially domestic shipping companies. Australia retained most ports in public ownership and concentrated on commercialization and corporatization. In contrast, New Zealand favored corporatization and partial privatization, with the majority of shares held by local authorities. In the United Kingdom, privatization limited rather than enhanced competition between ports (Saundry and Turnbull 1997).

A variety of ownership and management models is in use in South Asia. India, the country with the largest number of ports in operation, uses both the public service and the landlord models. Bangladesh has yet to introduce the landlord model at either of its main ports. Table 3.1 provides a summary of ownership and management models currently used at South Asian ports. Table 3.2 documents private sector involvement in South Asian ports as of 2014.

Figure 3.1  Risk-Sharing by Public and Private Sectors, by Type of Port Model

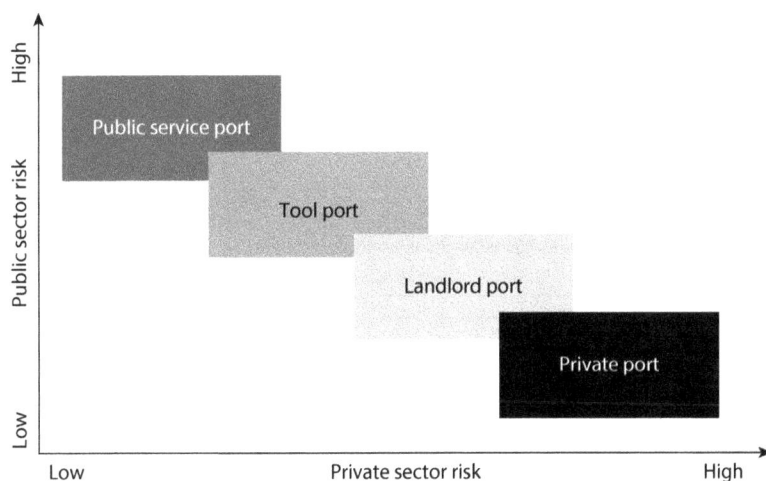

Table 3.1  Port Models in Use in South Asia

| Model | Ports |
| --- | --- |
| Landlord | Chennai, Cochin, JNPT, Kolkata, Mumbai, Mundra, Pipavav, Tuticorin, Visakhapatnam (India); Gwadar, Karachi, Qasim (Pakistan); Colombo (Sri Lanka) |
| Tool | Chittagong (Bangladesh) |
| Public service | Mongla (Bangladesh); Kandla, Mormugao, New Mangalore, Paradip (India); Malé (Maldives) |

**Table 3.2  Private Sector Involvement in South Asian Ports, 2014**

| Country | Port | Private operators | Date of concession |
|---|---|---|---|
| Bangladesh | Chittagong | None | n.a. |
| | Mongla | None | n.a. |
| India | Chennai | DP World | 2001 |
| | | PSA | 2006 |
| | Cochin | DP World and Concor | 2005 |
| | JNPT | DP World | 2000[a] |
| | | APM and Concor | 2004 |
| | | PSA | 2014[b] |
| | Kandla | None | n.a.[c] |
| | Kolkata | ABG and PSA | 2003[d] |
| | | PSA | 2014 |
| | | ULA | 2014[e] |
| | Mormugao | None | n.a. |
| | Mumbai | Gammon and Dragados | 2007 |
| | Mundra | DP World | 2003[f] |
| | | APSEZ | 2007 |
| | | MSC and APSEZ | 2013 |
| | | CMA and APSEZ | 2014[g] |
| | New Mangalore | None | n.a. |
| | Paradip | None | n.a. |
| | Pipavav | APM | 2005 |
| | Tuticorin | PSA and SICAL | 1999 |
| | | ABG | 2012 |
| | Visakhapatnam | DP World and ULA | 2003 |
| Pakistan | Qasim | DP World | 1995[h] |
| | Gwadar | China Overseas Port Holding (COPHC) | 2013 |
| | Karachi | Hutchison | 1998 |
| | | ICTSI and MGC | 2002[i] |
| | | Hutchison | 2007[j] |
| Sri Lanka | Colombo | SAGT (APM, John Keells, and others) | 1999 |
| | | China Merchant Holdings | 2010[k] |

*Sources:* Port authorities and container terminal operators' websites.

*Note:* n.a. = not applicable.

a. P&O Ports of Australia was the original concessionaire for the Nhava Sheva International Container Terminal in 2000. DP World acquired P&O Ports of Australia in 2006.

b. In early 2014 PSA was awarded a 30-year concession for the development and operation of the fourth container terminal at JNPT. The first phase is expected to start operating in 2018.

c. In 2006 private terminal operator ABG won a concession at the Port of Kandla. In 2012 the port "terminated the concession" after the firm failed to fulfill a key obligation regarding the contractually mandated minimum guaranteed volumes at the terminal.

d. In 2008 PSA bought 49 percent of ABG Kolkata Container Terminal, which operates two berths at the Netaji Subhas Docks in Kolkata. PSA sold its shares back to ABG Infralogistcs in January 2015, after being awarded a 10-year concession for the upgrade and operation of five berths at Netaji Subhas Docks. They started operating in November 2014, under the name Bharat Kolkata Container Terminals.

e. In 2014 the Kolkata Port Trust awarded United Liner Agency of India (ULA) a contract for the Haldia International Container Terminal.

f. This concession was originally awarded to P&O of Australia, which DP World acquired in 2006.

g. In mid-2014 APSEZ formed a joint venture with CMA to develop and operate the fourth container terminal at Mundra. It is expected to become operational in mid-2016.

h. This concession was originally awarded to P&O of Australia, which DP World acquired in 2006. DP World is building a second container terminal at the port.

i. An ICTSI subsidiary completed the acquisition of 35 percent of PICT in October 2012, subsequently increasing its stake to 64.5 percent.

j. Hutchinson, which operates the first concession of a container terminal at the Port of Karachi, was awarded the concession of the new South Asia Pakistan Terminal, which is expected to start operations by mid-2016.

k. Construction of the terminal started in December 2011; the first phase was ceremonially opened to traffic in August 2013.

## Status of Private Sector Involvement in Bangladesh, India, Pakistan, and Sri Lanka

The following subsections briefly overview private sector participation in the port sector in Bangladesh, India, Pakistan, and Sri Lanka.

### Bangladesh: Denying the Evidence

The ports of Chittagong and Mongla are managed by port authorities that report to the Ministry of Shipping, which provides overall sector policy guidance and some regulatory oversight.

The Chittagong Port Authority (CPA) has a monopoly position over international port facilities, including regulation of the private stevedores, who operate under short-term (typically three- to five-year) contracts with CPA.[1] The primary contractor for container handling is SAIF, whose activities are concentrated at the Chittagong Container Terminal and the New Moorings Container Terminal. Other private operators provide container-handling services at the general cargo berths.[2] The CPA exercises a high degree of operational and financial autonomy, although major expenditures require approval from the ministry. The reasons for delays in making major decisions (such as buying cranes for the New Moorings Container Terminal, which was built in 2007) are not transparent.

The institutional setup at the CPA is not in line with best practices and does not meet the needs of an export-oriented economy. Alone among ports on the Indian subcontinent, Chittagong has not adopted the landlord model. Chittagong has considered concessions to international terminal operators in the past but has not actually granted them.

In the late 1990s, the U.S. stevedoring company SSA Marine requested permission to build a container terminal at Chittagong. The request was initially approved, but labor unions paralyzed the port with a string of protest strikes. SSA Marine then put the project on hold. It revived its plans and got them accepted when the government changed in 2001. In 2003, however, the trade unions went to the high court to challenge approval. They pursued the case on narrow grounds surrounding the legal status of the SSA Marine joint venture and won.

In 2010 the CPA initiated another bid for a concession. It drew up a shortlist of bidders that was reported by Lloyds List to include most of the top operators (PSA, APM Terminals, Hutchison, ICTSI). According to Lloyd's List, "there was some lobbying of the government and it was subsequently cancelled" (Lloyd's List n.d.) Bangladesh is the only country on the Indian subcontinent in which the private sector does not play a meaningful role in the container port sector.

### India: Tampering with Reform

India has undertaken initiatives to enhance the attractiveness of private sector investment since 1996, when it took the first steps toward liberalizing the port sector. The impact of these initiatives has been uneven. Reforms for the introduction of private participation were initiated in 1996 through the first policy guidelines for private sector participation. The public-private partnership (PPP) regime became more structured, organized, and predictable only after 2007, when a new model concession agreement was developed to serve as a guideline document for drafting concession agreements.

PPP project award and implementation have been marked by delays and disputes that arise from various policy-related constraints at the pre- and post-award stages (Raghuram and Shukla 2014). About five years are required to obtain all clearances (including environmental clearance) from the government and appropriate ministries before financial closure can be achieved and construction started; another three to four years are needed before a port becomes operational (Port Finance India and Ernst & Young 2012). The preparation of vision statements, investment plans, and a maritime agenda have not been sufficient to achieve investment targets. Only about half the investments targeted in the 12th five-year plan were achieved, with private investment accounting for about a third of the target (table 3.3).

Leveraging private sector investment for port development is a key theme in India and is marked by numerous ongoing initiatives. As of September 2013, 58 port projects with private investment were ongoing, with total investment of $11 billion. Another 83 port projects with private investment were under consideration or in the initial stages of development, with planned investment of $23 billion.

As more and more options for cargo handling emerge along the coastline, the need for greater capacity in hinterland connections and interlinkages among them is rising. The government has introduced a slew of initiatives to encourage investment in last-/first-mile railway and road links (through PPPs) and development of multimodal logistics parks.

### Pakistan: Embracing Landlord Port Reforms

All three of Pakistan's ports are administered by port trusts/authorities under the Ministry of Ports and Shipping. They have, however, made steady progress toward adopting the landlord port model. Almost all containers, which account for the vast majority of Pakistan's international trade in terms of value, are handled at terminals with international operators (Hutchison, ICTSI, and DP World). Port Qasim has operated almost entirely as a landlord port since it

**Table 3.3  Planned versus Actual Investment in India under 10th, 11th, and 12th Five-Year Plans**
*(millions of dollars, except where otherwise indicated)*

| | 10th plan (2002–07) | | 11th plan (2007–12) | | 12th plan (2012–17) |
|---|---|---|---|---|---|
| Actor | Actual investment | Projected investment | Actual investment | Difference between projected and actual investment (percent) | Projected investment |
| Central government | 438 | 4,981 | 913 | 82 | 3,445 |
| State governments | 153 | 605 | 460 | 24 | 927 |
| Private sector | 3,134 | 9,080 | 6,050 | 33 | 28,591 |
| **Total** | **3,725** | **14,665** | **7,423** | **49** | **32,964** |

*Source:* Ministry of Shipping of India 2014.

opened in 1980, serving the steel, petroleum, chemical, and other industries. Almost all its bulks are handled at independent terminals, and it has a container terminal operated by DP World.

Until the 1990s, Karachi was a traditional South Asian port with old facilities, labor problems, low productivity, difficult landside access, and high charges. Over the last 20 years, it has made progress toward becoming a landlord port. In 1997 it became the first port on the Indian subcontinent to set up a privately operated container terminal (KICT, run by Hutchinson). When the deep water South Asia Pakistan Terminal opens, in 2016, it will have three competing terminals.

Reform lost momentum after 2007: Staff levels have risen, and no further concession or privatization has occurred. The Karachi Port Trust's current mission statement commits the port to further reforms, however, vowing to "lease out port infrastructure, land, access and assets to private port operators on a long-term basis while retaining regulatory functions." Between 1997 and 2007, Karachi reduced employment from 13,000 to 4,000. By 2014 it had increased by more than 40 percent, to 5,700. In contrast, Port Qasim employs fewer than 2,000 people; Rotterdam, the largest port in Europe, employs only 1,100 people.

The combination of reasonable staff levels at private terminals and over-manning at the port authority is common throughout the Indian subcontinent. Overstaffing is a legacy of the past, when port operations were operated by port authorities and cargo handling was labor intensive. Older port authorities have made slow progress in reducing staff. For example, the old Port of Mumbai had more than 17,000 employees in 2011 and the Port of Chennai had almost 8,000 employees, far more than the 1,700 at the new and busier Port of JNPT.

Further implementation of the landlord port model in Karachi would introduce private sector participation in the provision of ancillary services and bulk cargo handling. Pilotage is retained by the port authorities in many other ports that are fundamentally landlord ports, but a shift to private towage, dredging, and bulk cargo handling would be in line with best practice in ports worldwide. The strong labor unions in Karachi have been able to resist rationalization programs.

### Sri Lanka: Bringing Private Sector to Spur Growth

All four ports in Sri Lanka are governed by the Sri Lanka Ports Authority (SLPA), which was set up by an Act of Parliament in 1979 to be the owner, operator, and sole supplier of marine and cargo-handling services at the country's ports. Colombo's traffic stagnated for several years in the late 1990s, mainly because of its low efficiency, lack of effective capacity, and increasing congestion. Until 1999 SLPA ran all operations, including the Jaya Container Terminal. Since then it has carried out significant reforms, introducing concessions for the operation of container terminals. The SAGT terminal, set up by P&O Ports and a local trader under a 30-year concession agreement, was the first terminal with private

Competitiveness of South Asia's Container Ports • http://dx.doi.org/10.1596/978-1-4648-0892-0

participation in Colombo. In 2011 China Merchant Holdings won the concession for the Colombo South Container Terminal.[3]

The government has actively sought private sector participation in the development of port infrastructure through partnerships in the form of either build-own-operate (BOO) or build-operate-transfer (BOT) transactions. In 2006 the Cabinet Subcommittee on Investment Promotion established a PPP unit within the Board of Investment. The Asian Development Bank has partly financed the development of the Colombo South Port. The private sector will finance the terminals, such as the Colombo South Container Terminal. China Merchants Holdings (CMHI) and the China Harbor Engineering Company are constructing a terminal at the Port of Hambantota, at a cost of $600 million.[4] Whether it is successful remains to be seen. It is expected that the Chinese company will hold a majority share of the joint venture with SLPA. The concession is for 35 years, with the option of extending the contract for a further 5 years.

Since the opening of the first terminal concession at Colombo, progress in port reform has been mixed. The Asia Development Bank offered to finance the $400 million breakwater that was necessary to expand the South Harbor on several conditions, including corporatization of the state-run container terminal (the Jaya Container Terminal); further progress toward a landlord port model, with additional concession to private operators (opposed by the unions); and changes in the legal framework. None of these conditions has been implemented.[5]

### Relationship between Private Sector Participation and Performance

Performance of landlord ports in South Asia varies widely, but most such ports perform better than the few remaining public and tool ports.[6] Operational performance in South Asia supports the global evidence on the positive influence of port models marked by the separation of overall port oversight, regulation, and basic infrastructure provision from dedicated operational management, investment, and execution.

Some landlord ports, such as JNPT and Colombo, clearly performed better than public service and tool ports (figure 3.2). For others, such as Cochin and Tuticorin, performance depends on the metric used.

In the case of economic efficiency, or efficiency in the use of port facilities, large and medium-size landlord ports clearly performed better than public ports on average. Mundra, which was developed from the outset as a landlord port, is one of the most dynamic container ports in South Asia. Its throughput grew by more than 30 percent a year on average since it started operating, in 2003. Older or more mature ports, such as Mumbai and Kandla, nevertheless fare better than Mundra in the benchmark in panel a in figure 3.2, because Mundra is much newer and still expanding. Its efficiency in the use of port facilities increased by 10 times since it started operating (see chapter 2); by 2010 it already showed an efficiency score significantly higher than that of Kandla or Mumbai.

**Figure 3.2  Economic and Operational Performance at Selected South Asian Ports**

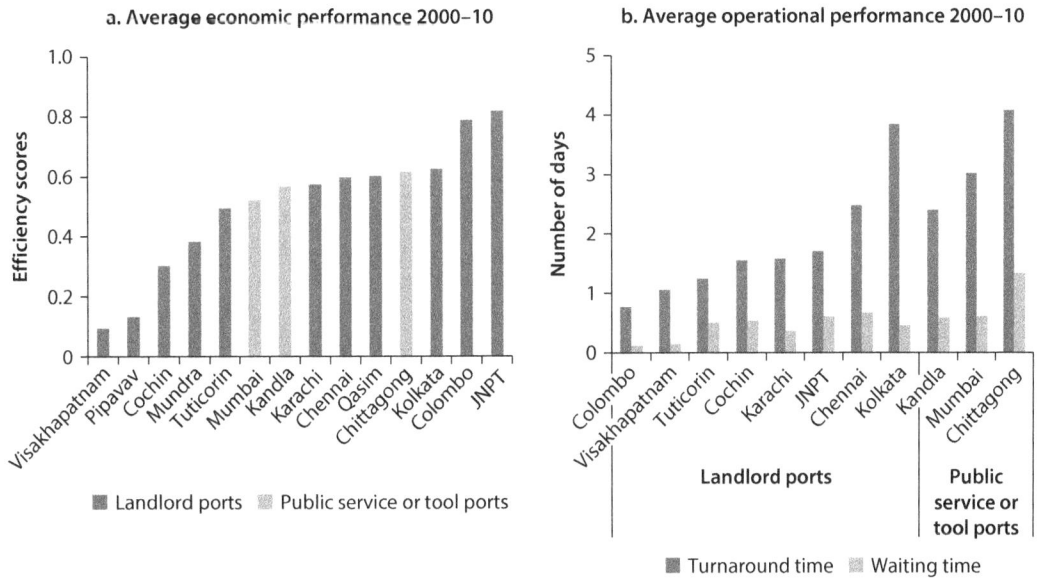

a. Average economic performance 2000–10

b. Average operational performance 2000–10

Landlord ports   Public service or tool ports

Turnaround time   Waiting time

*Note:* Efficiency scores refer to efficiency in use of port facilities (pure efficiency, as defined in chapter 2). Chittagong, Kandla, and Mumbai were public service or tool ports for at least six years between 2000 and 2010.

Chittagong, the only port in South Asia that has never been a landlord port, presents a dichotomy. The port's operational performance is the worst in the region, but it is not a bad performer with regard to efficiency in the use of its facilities. The lack of investments in Chittagong and the growth in exports of ready-made garments in Bangladesh have forced the port to operate almost at capacity, making the most of the limited facilities it has. These facts explain the port's above-average efficiency in the use of its facilities and the very high turnaround and preberthing waiting times.

Higher levels of private sector participation in container ports are related to better port performance. As figure 3.3 indicates, the level of private sector participation (measured by the amount invested) is positively correlated with average efficiency in the use of port facilities and operational measures of performance, such as turnaround and preberthing waiting times. Larger investments allow port operators to expand and improve berths and terminals, buy modern and better cranes, and install better information and management systems to optimize operations. Achieving internationally or regionally competitive operational standards generally requires private sector participation. However, private sector participation on its own need not achieve benchmark standards unless an enabling environment, including the proper design of concessions, is in place. The evidence from South Asia is telling, as discussed in the following sections.

**Figure 3.3  Relationship between Private Sector Participation and Port Efficiency in South Asia**

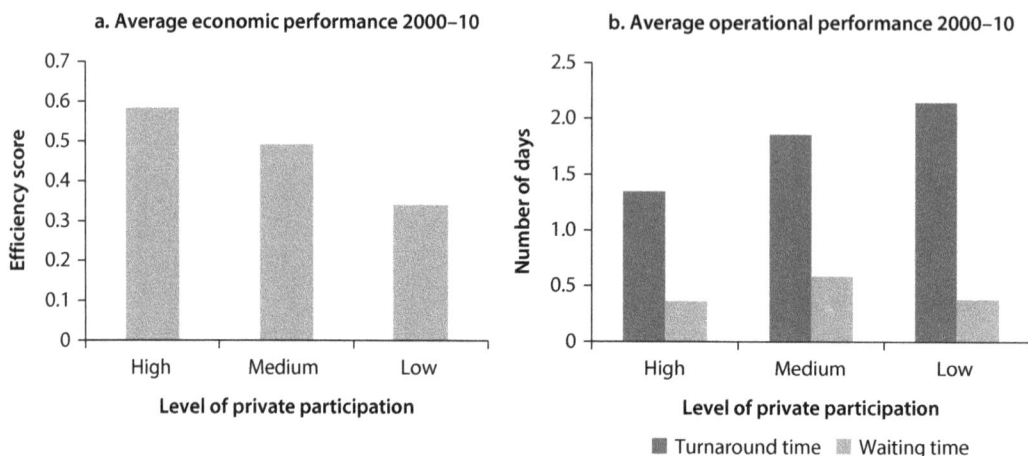

a. Average economic performance 2000–10

b. Average operational performance 2000–10

■ Turnaround time   ▨ Waiting time

*Source:* PPIAF database and performance indicators from chapter 2.
*Note:* Efficiency scores refer to efficiency in use of port facilities (pure efficiency, as defined in chapter 2). Only ports that had private sector participation for at least six years during this period are considered. Level of private participation refers to the dollar amount invested by the private sector.

## Do Port Governance Characteristics Affect Port Performance?

Institutions in infrastructure sectors have traditionally received little attention from a public governance angle. Most public sector analysis has focused on institutions and public management tools located at the center of government. Policies such as public financial and budget management, civil service reform, access to information and participation laws, and results-based management have traditionally been led by either the ministers of finance or the highest administrative level of government (prime minster or president). Sectors responsible for the delivery of public services were left unattended in terms of their institutional development.

From the perspective of service delivery, governance can be understood as the set of incentives and accountabilities that affect the way provider organizations, their managers, and staffs behave, as well as the quality and efficiency with which they deliver services (Fiszbein, Ringold, and Rogers 2011). The interphase between institutional design and the delivery of services requires the development of new frameworks of analyses and a more dynamic view of governance that allows a better understanding of why some sectors behave differently from others.

Port authorities have emerged as fundamental determinants of port performance. A professionalized governing authority, a well-placed strategic plan, and a competent bureaucracy are critical aspects of good long-term planning and management of ports. The gains of sound port planning can be considerable: Roy and Koster (2012) estimate that bad yard planning can raise handling time by up to 30 percent. Port users of the Virginia Port Authority (VPA) stress that stability in port governance and leadership is vital because it provides some certainty regarding the decisions of a port's current and prospective customers (JLARC 2013). The consensus is that ports should be led by a group of professionals who share rich relevant expertise.

The low-quality infrastructure and low efficiency of most ports in South Asia call for urgent improvements in the management of port authorities (Wilson and Otsuki 2007). A report from the National Transport Development Policy Committee of India (2014) emphasizes the need for change. It recommends the corporatization of port authorities and the decentralization of management, following the steps of state-owned enterprises in other sectors in India.

Despite the importance of port governance, the issue remains understudied in South Asia. Limited efforts have been made to understand the role of boards of directors, the use of strategic planning, the relationship between the overall institutional quality of the government and the governance of ports, and the assessment of the performance of port authorities. This section takes a first step into this uncharted area.

### Measuring the Governance of Boards in South Asia

A board governance index (BGI) was developed to measure different aspects of the governance of port authority boards in South Asia. In Mundra and Pipavav, the only nonmajor ports in India, the light touch regulation in place in Gujarat grants the private developer/operator of the port the right to make decisions in areas that are the responsibility of the port authority in other landlord ports. Consequently, for the purpose of the analysis in this section, the developer/operator is considered to be the port authority for these ports.

The BGI is made up of five components: professionalization, transparency of appointments, composition, number of members, and renewability of mandate. Table 3.4 presents the rationale for each component.

The BGI is the simple average of all five variables, the scores for which range from 0 (worst performance) to 1 (best performance). Information about components 2–5 was collected by analyzing the legal statutes of each port authority.

**Table 3.4 Rationale behind Components of Board Governance Index**

| Component | Rationale |
| --- | --- |
| Professionalization | Boards of professionals make independent and more rational decisions than boards made up of poorly educated members. |
| Transparency of appointments | An open process of appointments allows the engagement of port users, the community, and trade associations whose interests are at stake in major ports' decisions. |
| Composition | Boards that include members from the private sector make better decisions than boards made only of public sector representatives. |
| Number of members | Smaller boards are more efficient than larger ones. |
| Renewability of mandate | Boards with limited terms bring new air and thinking. Board members with indefinite mandates can stagnate decisions and prioritize their own interests over those of the port. |

**Figure 3.4	Board Governance Index of Selected Ports**

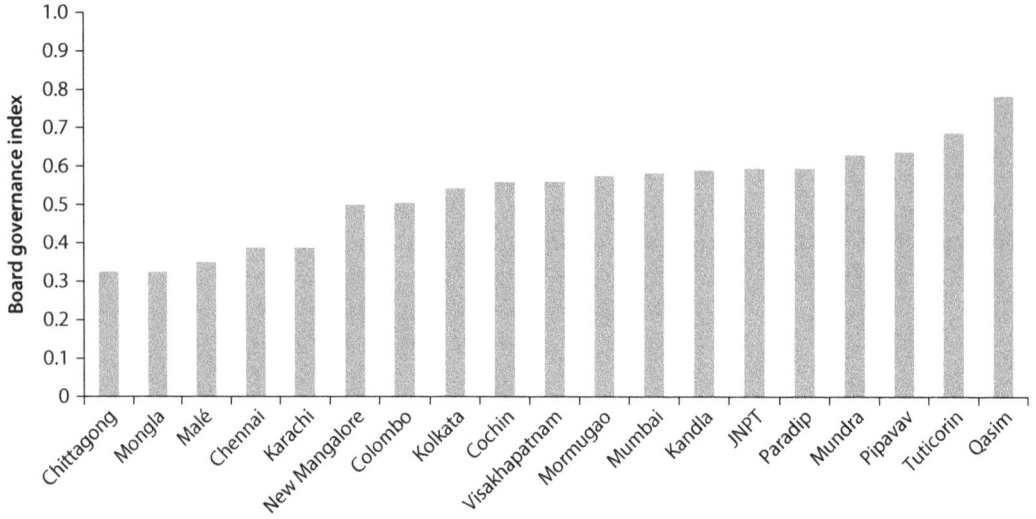

*Note:* Indexes range from 0 (worst performance) to 1 (best performance).

Information for component 1 was obtained from port authorities' websites, professional webpages with self-reported and publicly available information (such as LinkedIn), and journals.

Results from the BGI analysis show a common set of patterns (figure 3.4). Top boards show high levels of professionalization and levels of private sector participation that are average or above average for the region. The two Indian nonmajor ports in the sample (Mundra and Pipavav) are among the top six performers. In terms of the professionalization of boards, these ports do not differ significantly from public trusts. Particularly in India, the boards of port authorities show high levels of education and professional experience. The main difference between the ports of Mundra and Pipavav and traditional public port authorities is the presence of independent members. Inclusion of independent board members has become a common feature of corporate governance in India for both the public and the private sectors.

Higher private investment seems to enhance board governance, possibly because boards need to make more complex and challenging decisions when private enterprises are partners or counterparts at the port. The case of state-owned enterprises with minor private ownership provides an interesting example in this regard. As the private sector engages in the decision-making process of state-owned enterprises, the members of the board representing the majority of shares start facing higher levels of control and oversight. Governments therefore need to appoint better-skilled members to the board (or board members need to acquire relevant skills).

The governance of the Karachi Port Trust, which has a low BGI, has been criticized by port users as ineffective. A key feature that is out of line with best international practice is the significant intervention by the Ministry of Ports and Shipping in daily operational and financial matters. Despite the law granting rights to the board rather than the ministry, board chairs have naval or civil service backgrounds rather than commercial or maritime experience. Their tenures are not long enough for them to pick up the experience necessary to guide the port.

### Regional and Country Assessments of Boards

The best governance attribute of boards of directors at the regional level is the openness of their appointment procedures. About 70 percent of port authorities conduct public consultations before appointing board members (figure 3.5). This practice is standard at Indian ports. In the other countries examined, boards with fewer members and more significant engagement of members from the nongovernmental sector seem to perform best.

The second most important regional attribute of boards is their level of professionalization. More than 60 percent of the statues of port authorities establish qualification criteria for appointment to the board of directors. Members of the boards of selected ports also show high educational levels.

Indian boards outperform their regional counterparts in transparency of appointments and professionalization of their members. Other research identifies the professionalization of boards as the greatest contributor to the performance of public enterprises (Andrés, Guasch and López Azumendi 2011). Board members at Indian ports show the highest educational levels. For the other countries analyzed, professionalization lags other components of the BGI (figure 3.6). Higher levels of professionalization at Indian ports could explain better management and better performance of port authorities there than in the rest of the region.

**Figure 3.5  Components of Board Governance in South Asia**

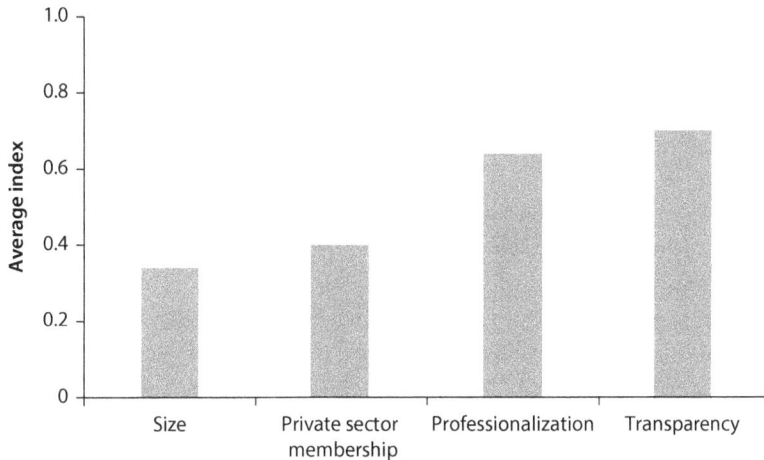

*Note:* Indexes range from 0 (worst performance) to 1 (best performance).

**Figure 3.6  Components of Board Governance of Ports in India and the Rest of South Asia**

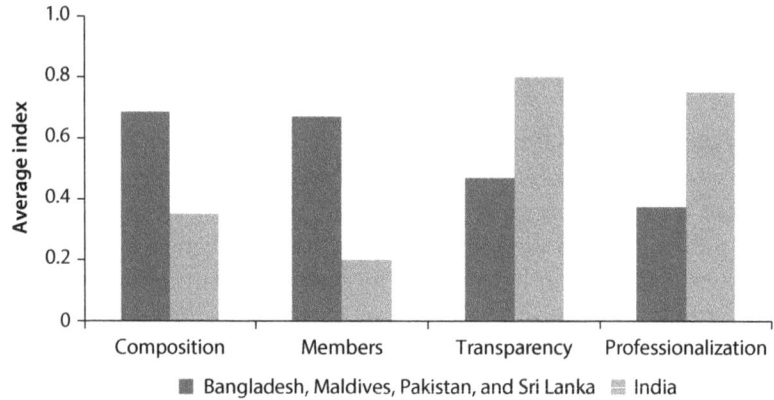

*Note:* Indexes range from 0 (worst performance) to 1 (best performance).

**Figure 3.7  Board Governance Index and Efficiency of South Asian Ports**

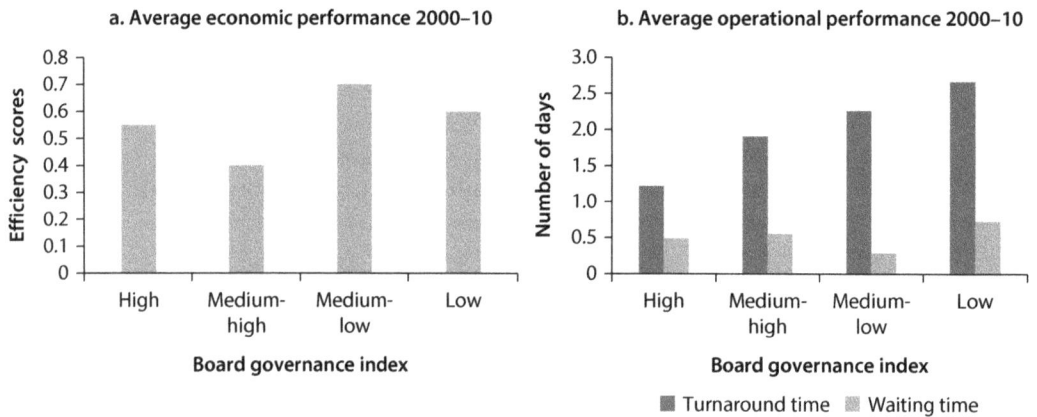

*Note:* Efficiency scores refer to efficiency in use of port facilities (pure efficiency, as defined in chapter 2).

### Relationship between Board Governance and Performance

Figure 3.7 shows the relationship between the average performance of South Asian container ports and the BGI. The relationship with economic efficiency is not clear, but the relationship between the BGI and operational performance is strong: Ports with higher BGIs have shorter average turnaround times and preberthing waiting times. These relationships may reflect the fact that the board of directors of port authorities in landlord ports—the large majority in South Asia—have more influence or control over ancillary services, such as tugging, pilotage, freight forwarding, customs, and accessibility to the port (that is, connectivity with the domestic transport network) through investments in last-/first-mile connectivity. Ancillary services and port accessibility have a stronger impact on operational performance than economic performance.

Chittagong's port authority has a very low BGI. Exports take twice as long to load as imports at the Chittagong Container Terminal, largely because of lack of enforcement of official cutoffs for exports and an inadequate tariff scheme on container stacking. Wasteful transfer of containerized goods into covered vans for transport to Dhaka and vice versa is common (in most countries containers go door to door). Dwell times for containers (the time spent in port) averaged 17 days in 2012. The figure is lower than it was in 2005 (25 days) but still many times longer than the 3–4 days typical at efficient ports. As a result, the backup area is highly congested and vehicle traffic chaotic. According to shipping lines and other port users, the main reasons for these patterns include complicated customs procedures, slow processing of documentation and payments by importers, poor connectivity with Dhaka, and vested interests.

## Does Competition Improve Port Performance?

Captive port traffic, barriers to establish new ports and enter the terminal market, tariff regulation, and the high concentration in the port operator market, among other factors, have traditionally limited competition in the port industry. The lack of competitive pressures affects the performance of a port. South Asia's port sector has also experienced major changes in its structure, with greenfield ports becoming major players in the market for container traffic. All of these changes are likely to affect the competition landscape in the sector.

The literature on port competition started to expand at the same time the containerization process did, in the mid-1990s.[7] The spectacular growth of East Asian economies at the end of the last century meant that the focus was on East Asian ports;[8] however, little attention was devoted to the South Asian port sector.

This section aims to identify the state of the art of the sources of competition in South Asian container ports and their relationship with port performance. Geographic location, proximity to competitors, type of cargo, and specialization in transshipment traffic have significant effects on the level of interport competition.[9] The existence of multiple terminals, the level of their physical capital, and the nature of the terminal operators affect intraport competition (competition within the port). Table 3.5 summarizes the measures used in the analysis as well as the hypotheses and rationale behind them.

### Interport Competition
#### Country Market Shares
A port is considered to have market power when it is able to behave independently of its consumers and competitors to an appreciable extent.[10] A common measure of market power is market share (OECD 2011): Large market share is generally indicative of market power.

The market for container traffic shows high levels of concentration in all countries in South Asia. Sri Lanka and Bangladesh are the most concentrated markets, with Colombo handling 100 percent of container traffic in Sri Lanka and Chittagong handling more than 92 percent in Bangladesh. Pakistan's market

**Table 3.5  Measures, Hypotheses, and Rationales for Assessment of Competition at Ports**

| Measure | Hypothesis | Rationale |
|---|---|---|
| Country market share | Higher levels of concentration lead to lower levels of competition. | Ports that continuously enjoy higher market shares for a long period face lower competition. |
| Geographic concentration | The greater the number of ports that serve the same hinterland and are managed by different terminal operators, the greater the competition among them. | The existence of ports competing for the same hinterland increases competition when these ports are managed by different terminal operators. |
| Containerization | Ports with large shares of containerization face greater competitive pressures. | International logistics networks and globalization of container liners create competition among specialized ports in the fight to attract and retain shipping companies. |
| Transshipment | Ports with high transshipment levels face greater international competitive pressures. | Port competition relies not only on neighboring facilities but also on international hubs. As the hinterland may not be of relevance, ports struggle to maximize efficiency and minimize costs to better serve deep-sea traffic needs. |
| Intraport market structure | Ports with more than one terminal managed by different operators face greater competition. | The more terminals operated by different companies, the more competitive the environment at the port. |

is a duopoly, with Karachi capturing more than 60 percent of container traffic and Qasim capturing the remaining 40 percent (Gwadar, the third port in Pakistan, has not attracted any cargo since its opening in 2007); these shares have remained stable for the past 20 years. India's container market is also concentrated, with JNPT capturing almost 40 percent. Since Mundra and Pipavav opened, in the early 2000s, the two ports have captured 29 percent of the Indian container market, taking share away primarily from Mumbai, JNPT, and Kandla (figure 3.8).

### Geographical competition: The role of hinterland and terminal operators

The more ports operated by different terminal operators serving the same hinterland, the greater the competition for cargo to and from the hinterland. Expansion of the port sector across the world has shifted the port industry from an environment with captive hinterland advantages to one of contestable hinterland (García and Sánchez 2006).

Inland connectivity between South Asian ports and their hinterlands is generally poor. All countries face congestion on roads and rail for inland cargo movements. All countries are trying to improve inland connectivity, but progress is slow. As a result, although inland markets are contestable in theory, competition in South Asia is more restricted than in more developed regions.

In Bangladesh there is almost no competition between Chittagong and Mongla. The shallow waters at Mongla, together with the limited handling capacity and connectivity with the main economic centers in the country, remove it from consideration by shippers in Bangladesh. In terms of distance, Kolkata and some of the other Indian ports along the eastern coast, which are close to Chittagong and Mongla, could compete for the same hinterland.

**Figure 3.8 Market Shares of Indian Ports, 2000 and 2013**
*percent*

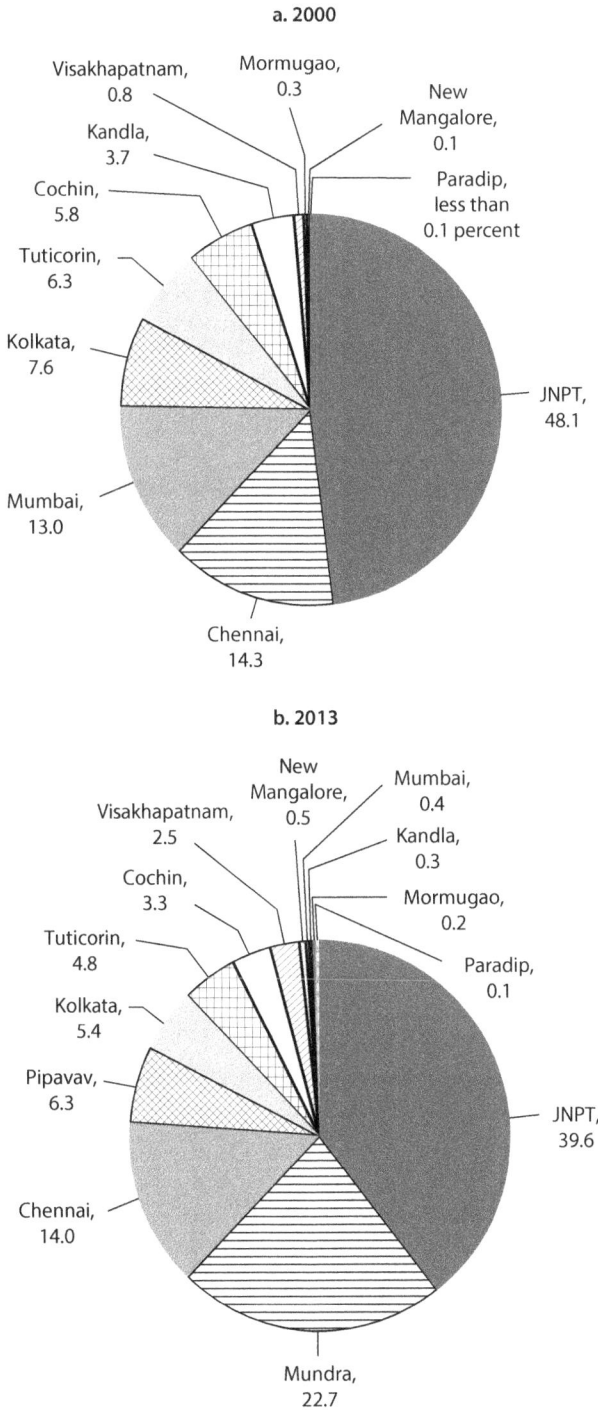

a. 2000

Visakhapatnam, 0.8
Mormugao, 0.3
New Mangalore, 0.1
Kandla, 3.7
Paradip, less than 0.1 percent
Cochin, 5.8
Tuticorin, 6.3
Kolkata, 7.6
JNPT, 48.1
Mumbai, 13.0
Chennai, 14.3

b. 2013

New Mangalore, 0.5
Mumbai, 0.4
Visakhapatnam, 2.5
Kandla, 0.3
Cochin, 3.3
Mormugao, 0.2
Tuticorin, 4.8
Paradip, 0.1
Kolkata, 5.4
Pipavav, 6.3
JNPT, 39.6
Chennai, 14.0
Mundra, 22.7

*Sources:* Ministry of Road Transport and Highways of India 2014, port authorities' websites, and World Development Indicators databases.

Competitiveness of South Asia's Container Ports • http://dx.doi.org/10.1596/978-1-4648-0892-0

However, lengthy delays at border crossings and the lack of free transit of trucks between the countries prevents real hinterland competition between Indian and Bangladeshi ports. A similar issue arises between ports in Pakistan and ports in the northwest of India: Although they are less than 250 nautical miles from Karachi and Qasim, Kandla and Mundra do not compete for the hinterland because of transit and trade limitations between the two countries.

The Indian west coast shows significantly greater competition over hinterland than the east coast. Ports on the west coast handle 73 percent of container cargo, with the five ports in Gujarat and Maharashtra (JNPT, Kandla, Mumbai, Mundra, and Pipavav) handling 69 percent of India's traffic. These ports can be divided into two main clusters: Kandla and Mundra, which are next to each other, and Mumbai, JNPT, and Pipavav, with Pipavav less than 200 nautical miles from Mumbai and JNPT. The third-largest cluster of ports is in the South of India, where Tuticorin and Cochin handle just over 8 percent of container cargo. Chennai alone handles more than this cluster (14 percent). Its closest competing port, Tuticorin, is about 350 nautical miles.[11]

Terminal operators play a significant role in competition among ports. Most of the large port terminal operators in the world operate container terminals in the region. India has opened the door to more operators than other countries in the region (figure 3.9). However, DP World, with terminals (in joint venture or alone) in the three busiest container ports in India (JNPT, Chennai, and Mundra), captures close to half the container market in the country. It is also the largest operator in Pakistan and South Asia as a whole. Both DP World and APM (the second-largest operator in the region) work in partnership with large shipping liners, and so they are likely to attract more container traffic to their specialized terminals. In India only Chennai, Tuticorin, and Visakhapatnam have no competing operators within 200 nautical miles; for cargo to and from the hinterland, they therefore face the least competition among Indian ports. In Pakistan and in the two clusters in the northwest of India, competition is more intense, as there are more than two operators within less than 100 nautical miles.

Sri Lanka and Pakistan are at the opposite ends of the spectrum. The Port of Colombo faces no competition. It faces more pressure from transshipment of deep-sea traffic than from the domestic market. Interport competition comes from hub ports in the Indian and Western Pacific Oceans. In Pakistan, Karachi and Qasim, which are just 20 nautical miles apart, compete for the same hinterland—the entire country. Three private Operators—DP World, APM, and MGC—split the market for container handling almost evenly, creating a very competitive environment.[12]

### Containerization as a proxy for competition

Highly specialized container ports and terminals are heavily dependent on shipping liners. Containerization has led not only to greater integration of supply chains (Rodrigue 2013) but also to the establishment of a common competition framework among ports specializing in this type of cargo. The technological revolution of containerization has put continuous pressure on transport costs and given

**Figure 3.9 Operators' Shares of Container Throughput in South Asia, 2010**

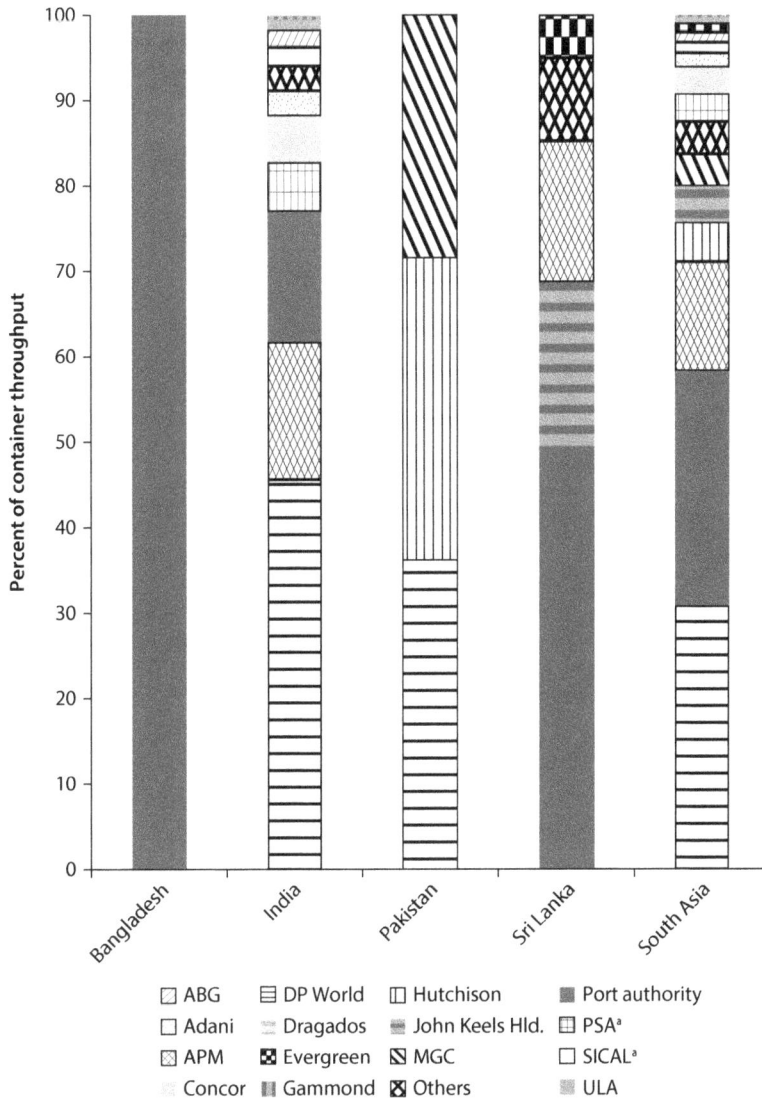

*Sources:* Ministry of Road Transport and Highways of India 2011, port authorities, and national ministries.
*Note:* Figures are based on TEUs and equity shares.
a. Total throughput from Chennai International Terminal was assigned to PSA, because SICAL sold its 40 percent share to PSA in June 2010.

increasing power to shipping alliances and large carriers (Limao and Venables 2001; Slack and Frémont 2009; Sys 2009). Logistic and value-added services have become strategic for the survival of ports (Juang and Roe 2010). Containerization led to the development of logistic centers, free trade zones, and similar actions in the hinterlands of East Asian ports in order to obtain or sustain their attractiveness or competitiveness (Lee, Song, and Ducruet 2008). Ducruet and Notteboom (2012) suggest that the extent of containerization at ports can be used as a proxy

**Table 3.6  Share of Cargo Volume at Ports in South Asia That Is Containerized, 2013**

| Country | Port | Share of containerized shipping volume (percent) |
|---|---|---|
| Bangladesh | Chittagong | 22 |
| | Mongla | 36 |
| India | Chennai | 56 |
| | Cochin | 23 |
| | JNPT | 90 |
| | Kandla | 2 |
| | Kolkata | 25 |
| | Mormugao | 1 |
| | Mumbai | 1 |
| | Mundra | 40 |
| | New Mangalore | 2 |
| | Pipavav | 78 |
| | Tuticorin | 33 |
| | Visakhapatnam | 8 |
| Pakistan | Karachi | 26 |
| | Qasim | 41 |
| Sri Lanka | Colombo | 89 |

*Sources:* Based on data from Indian Ports Association, port authorities, and Sri Lanka Central Bank.

for the economic influence of maritime facilities, as ports compete not as individual places that handle ships but as crucial links within global supply chains (Hall and Jacobs 2010; Notteboom and Winkelmans 2001). A port with a higher containerization index can therefore be expected to face stronger competition.

Although only 22 percent of Indian cargo by volume is containerized (compared with 50 percent worldwide), the largest ports and the new players in the region are highly dependent on container traffic (table 3.6). Both JNPT and Colombo, leaders of traffic in the region, specialize almost exclusively in container traffic. Also highly dependent on container traffic are Mundra (40 percent of total cargo) and Pipavav (78 percent), two of the newest ports in Gujarat. Container traffic at Mundra is expected to increase, as two additional container terminals come into operation.[13] The development of specialized terminals along with the gradual adoption of container-handling technology at Chennai and Qasim put those ports on the South Asian container traffic map as well.

### The Role of Transshipment

Transshipment hubs are the facilities along international shipping networks where cargo is transferred from larger vessels to smaller vessels that serve the final ports of destination or another transshipment port. The distinction between hinterland and transshipment traffic means that two ports that do not serve the same hinterland may still operate in the same geographic market if they compete for the same transshipment traffic (OECD 2011).

**Table 3.7 Annual Share of Cargo Volume That Is Transshipped at Selected South Asian Ports, 2003–12**

| Port | 2003 | 2004 | 2005 | 2006 | 2007 | 2008 | 2009 | 2010 | 2011 | 2012 |
|------|------|------|------|------|------|------|------|------|------|------|
| Colombo | 66 | 66 | 67 | 73 | 73 | 76 | 76 | 75 | 73 | 73 |
| Cochin | 0 | 0 | 0 | 0 | 0 | 0 | 0 | 0 | 3 | 2 |
| Kandla | 0 | 0 | 0 | 1 | 3 | 2 | 0 | 2 | 1 | 0 |
| Kolkata | 5 | 6 | 6 | 5 | 5 | 5 | 4 | 2 | 2 | 1 |
| JNPT | 9 | 9 | 6 | 5 | 6 | 6 | 4 | 3 | 2 | 1 |
| Mumbai | 8 | 9 | 16 | 22 | 27 | 21 | 36 | 34 | 31 | 31 |
| Tuticorin | 0 | 0 | 0 | 0 | 0 | 0 | 3 | 0 | 3 | 2 |
| Visakhapatnam | 16 | 15 | 08 | 9 | 8 | 7 | 8 | 3 | 8 | 6 |

*Sources:* Based on data from Ministry of Road Transport and Highways of India 2013 and Sri Lanka Port Authority.
*Note:* Figures are based on volume. Only ports with some transshipment traffic over the period are included.

The level of competition among ports handling this kind of traffic is high, forcing ports—particularly terminals—to increase productivity and reduce prices (Rodrigue and Notteboom 2010). Pure transshipment hubs are highly vulnerable, because shipping lines can switch hubs if conditions make it favorable to do so (Wilmsmeier and Notteboom 2011). Ports handling both transshipment and gateway cargo face less risk of shipping lines switching ports (Notteboom, Parola, and Satta 2014).

Almost three-quarters of the containers handled at Colombo are transshipment boxes (table 3.7). It is the only South Asian port that competes directly with the main transshipment hubs of Singapore, Tanjung Pelepas, Port Klang, and Salalah. Colombo is particularly important for India, handling 13 percent of its containers. Transshipment is significantly less important at other South Asian ports.

### Intraport Competition

Intraport competition refers to competition among terminals within the same port, usually terminals run by different operators. Competition comes through pricing adjustments (for example, volume discounts) and service quality improvements (for example, preferential berth access). Clear evidence of competition would be shipping lines switching terminals at the same port.

Intraport competition is often restricted in South Asia, where 10 of 18 major ports have no intraport competition (table 3.8). Exceptions are the ports of Chennai, Colombo, JNPT, Karachi, Kolkata, Mumbai, Mundra, and Tuticorin, all of which have multiple terminals run by different operators. The Port of Karachi has seen intraport competition since the opening of its second terminal, in 2002, by a different operator.

Chennai, JNPT, Mundra, and Tuticorin all have multiple terminals run by different operators. The structure of competition at some of the other multiterminal ports is somewhat different. For example, the joint venture between Gammond and Dragados at the Indira Container Terminal in Mumbai competes with the port trust's operation of a second terminal. At the Port of Kolkata, the port trust

**Table 3.8  Port Facilities and Terminal Operators at Selected Ports in South Asia, 2014**

| Port | Terminal 1 | Terminal 2 | Terminal 3 | Terminal 4 |
|------|-----------|-----------|-----------|-----------|
| Qasim | DP World | n.a. | n.a. | n.a. |
| Chennai | DP World | PSA | n.a. | n.a. |
| Chittagong | Port authority | n.a. | n.a. | n.a. |
| Cochin | DP World and Concor | n.a. | n.a. | n.a. |
| Colombo | SAGT (APM and others)[a] | Port authority | Port authority | China Merchant Holdings[a] |
| Gwadar | China Overseas Holding | n.a. | n.a. | n.a. |
| JNPT | APM and Concor | Port authority | DP World | n.a. |
| Kandla | Port authority | n.a. | n.a. | n.a. |
| Karachi | Hutchison | ICTSI and MGC | n.a. | n.a. |
| Kolkata | ABG and PSA | Port authority | PSA | n.a. |
| Mongla | Port authority | n.a. | n.a. | n.a. |
| Mormugao | Port authority | n.a. | n.a. | n.a. |
| Mumbai | Port authority | Gammond and Dragados | n.a. | n.a. |
| Mundra | DP World | APSEZ | MSC and APSEZ | n.a. |
| New Mangalore | Port authority | n.a. | n.a. | n.a. |
| Pipavav | APM | n.a. | n.a. | n.a. |
| Tuticorin | PSA and Sical | ABG | n.a. | n.a. |
| Visakhapatnam | DP World and ULA | n.a. | n.a. | n.a. |

*Sources:* Port authority websites.
*Note:*
a. The Sri Lanka Port Authority holds 15 percent of the shares in the joint venture. n.a. = not applicable.

operates one terminal, and seven docks at the Netaji Subhas Docks are operated by the private sector (five of which are operated by PSA and two of which are operated by ABG). In Sri Lanka the port authority competes and partners with private operators. In Colombo intraport competition is introduced by different private operators as well as the port authority, which is the sole operator of the Jaya and Unity Container terminals and part of the joint ventures operating both the South Asia Gateway and the new Colombo South Container terminals. It is not uncommon for conflicts of interest to arise between the port trusts and the private sector when port trusts operate one or more terminals while competing with private terminal operators at the same port. The competition concern arises primarily as port trusts act both as regulators and as providers of commercial services in many instances, theoretically leading to a situation in which the landlord could refuses access to basic infrastructure to competing terminals.

### Competition Environment and Port Performance in South Asia

Based on the previous analysis, a competition index was developed to capture differences in the competitive environment in which container ports in South Asia operate. The analysis is based on the potential harm to competition, not the actual behavior of the parties involved. Anticompetitive behavior can arise in ports even if the competition environment is perceived as high, because of other barriers to competition.

The competition environment of a port is ranked as low (1), medium (2), or high (3) on each of the five measures described above, based on the criteria in table 3.9. The score for each port is the simple average of the five proxies (figure 3.10). Table B.1 categorizes each port along each dimension.

Competition in the container market is related to the performance of container ports in South Asia: On average, ports that operated in more competitive environments between 2000 and 2010 were more efficient in the use of their facilities than ports in less competitive environments (figure 3.11). On average, ships loading and offloading at ports that face the least competitive pressures waited longer to moor than ships at ports facing more competitive pressures. The total time ships spent at port was shorter the more competitive the environment the port operates. These results are in line with the intuition that ports operating in more competitive environments need to perform more efficiently in order to attract and retain traffic.

**Table 3.9  Criteria for Assessing Level of Competition at Ports**

| Measure | Low | Medium | High |
|---|---|---|---|
| Country market share (percent) | More than 25 | 10–25 | Less than 10 |
| Geographic concentration (nautical miles to port operated by different terminal operation) | More than 200 | 100–200 | Less than 100 |
| Containerization (percent of total traffic) | Less than 25 | 25–50 | More than 50 |
| Transshipment (percent of container traffic) | 0 | Less than 50 | More than 50 |
| Intraport market structure (number of operators for at least five years between 2000 and 2010) | One | Two | More than two |

*Note:* The intervals for hinterland competition were set based on the following assumptions: More than eight hours of navigation time to the next operator competing for common hinterland (a distance of more than 200 nautical miles) represents a low level of competition, 4–8 hours represents a medium level of competition, and less than four hours represents a high level of competition.

**Figure 3.10  Competition Environment Index of Selected South Asian Container Ports**

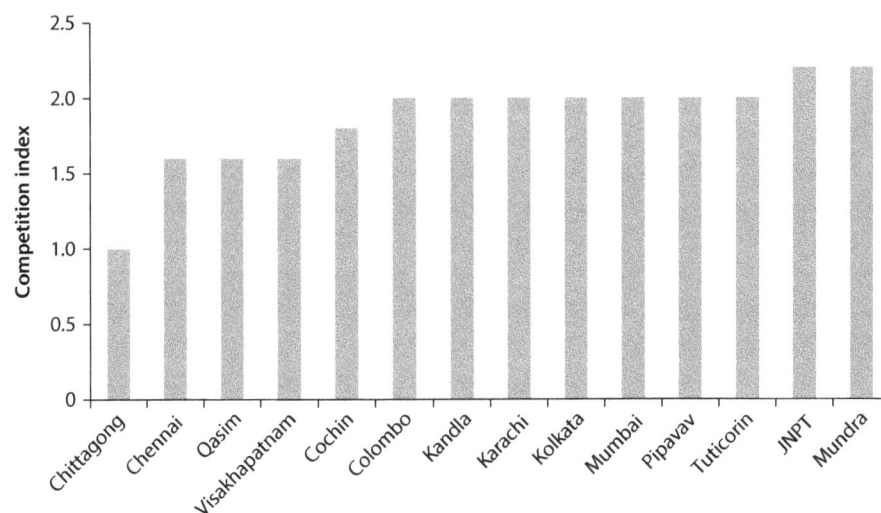

*Note:* Index is based on performance between 2000 and 2010.

**Figure 3.11  Competition Environment and Efficiency of South Asian Ports**

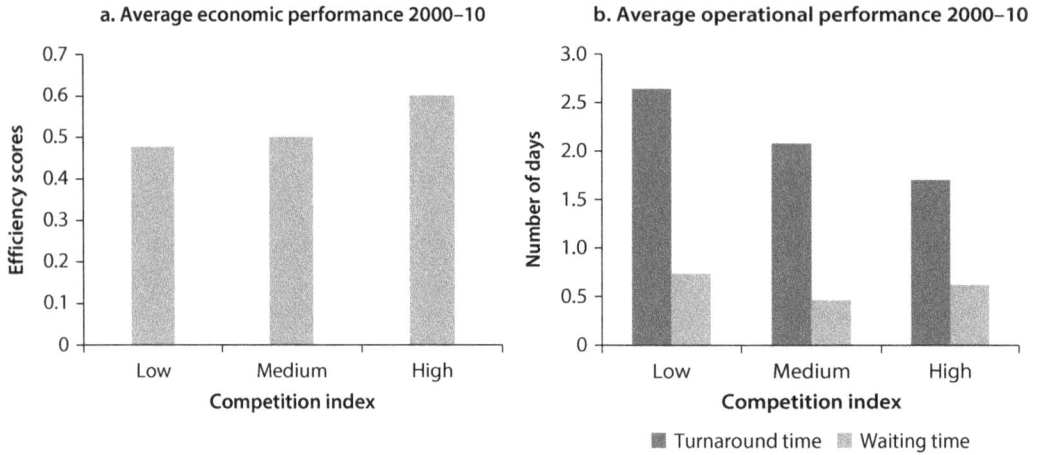

**a. Average economic performance 2000–10**

**b. Average operational performance 2000–10**

■ Turnaround time   ▨ Waiting time

*Note:* Efficiency scores refer to the efficiency in the use of port facilities (pure efficiency, as defined in chapter 2).

## Concluding Remarks

There has been improvement and modernization in the South Asian port sector, but more needs to be done to meet the growth and competitiveness challenge, especially in Bangladesh, India, and Pakistan. Policy makers could consider the following results in crafting sector development and reform.

### Takeaways on Private Sector Participation and Port Performance

Global evidence indicates that ports marked by the separation of overall port oversight, regulation, basic infrastructure provision and dedicated operational management, investment, and execution (the landlord model) perform better than other ports. Execution of this model has been mixed in South Asia. Reforms that promote higher levels of private sector participation are associated with better investment execution, better capital utilization, and an operational premium. Failure to adopt appropriate reforms puts South Asian ports at a disadvantage relative to ports in other regions.

Achieving international or regionally competitive performance generally requires private sector participation. But private sector participation on its own need not lead to better outcomes without an enabling environment that includes proper design of concessions. The preferred mode of private sector participation is through transparent, well-designed internationally competitive, long-term (at least 25-year) concessions, not through short-term contracts to private stevedores, as is the case in Bangladesh. The full benefits of private sector participation are most likely to be realized when the incentives are strongly weighted toward the market and operators are given a high level of control. The approach to tariff-setting and control should be light touch, structured to reflect the degree of competition in the market—a very different approach from the one adopted by India's major ports. Enhancing port performance by encouraging private sector participation through a well-developed enabling environment, including further adoption of the landlord port model, seems to be appropriate in South Asia.

### Takeaways on Port Governance and Port Performance

Port authorities have emerged as fundamental determinants of port performance. A professionalized governing authority, a well-placed strategic plan, and a competent bureaucracy are critical aspects of good long-term port planning and management. The consensus is that ports should be led by a group of professionals who share an abundance of relevant expertise.

The governance of port authority boards in South Asia is mixed. Top boards are highly professional and include independent members. They also tend to be found at ports that implemented the landlord port model and at which there is a significant level of private participation. The analysis reveals a strong and clear relationship between operational performance and board governance. Better boards seem to understand the complexity of port operations and the importance of well-functioning ancillary services and connectivity with the hinterland to ensure timely and efficient movement of cargo through the port. South Asian governments should consider strengthening the governance of port authority boards through increased professionalization of directors, an open process of appointments, and inclusion of independent members, among other factors, to create an environment that is conducive to better port performance.

### Takeaways on Competition and Port Performance

Stimulating competition (and at times the threat of entry) improves economic and operational performance. The logic is simple: Increased competition fuels efficiency improvements and productivity growth and can keep prices down.

Evidence suggests that new ports and more terminal operators at a port can improve the performance of existing operators—as has indeed happened in northwest India and in Sri Lanka. Competition is stimulated at the initial concession stage (through open bidding) and through port policy objectives that introduce new operators as port expansion proceeds. This process has occurred in India, Pakistan, and Sri Lanka. In contested hinterlands, such as northwest India, interport competition is a powerful force for improving port operation and investment. In the transshipment market segments, competition is often intense, motivating ports to perform at the production frontier.

Intra- and interport competition conditions at South Asian ports are mixed. Competition is essentially absent in Bangladesh, where the ministry and the port authority own and regulate the port sector and private sector participation is highly restricted.

Interport competition in India is limited by the chronic capacity shortfall. Although the recession "corrected" this situation in the short term, cargo volumes are expected to return to a growth path in the medium to long term. Interport competition is likely to emerge only over time, as capacity build-up is enabled through further policy and regulatory reform. Major ports are subject to tariff regulation by the Tariff Authority for Major Ports (TAMP); nonmajor ports have tariff-setting flexibility. Subject to tariff caps, major ports are unable to offer customized services. As a result, they are less competitive than nonmajor ports. Reform of tariff-setting—ideally in way that phases out intrusive tariff-setting by a regulator in favor of market-based tariffs where there is competition—would create a level playing field for major and nonmajor ports.

True intraport competition exists at JNPT and Mundra, where different firms operate different terminals. At other Indian ports, competition is absent; port authorities handle all terminal operations at Kandla, Mumbai, and other ports. At still others (such as Kolkata), port trusts effectively compete with the private sector. In Pakistan there is no intraport competition at Qasim. The Port of Karachi is so close, however, that the operator at Qasim actually competes with both operators at Karachi. In Sri Lanka the main interport competitors for Colombo are Singapore, Tanjung Pelepas, and Port Klang. Intraport competition has had a significant impact on Colombo's performance since the introduction of competition from private sector operators in the late 1990s.

### The Need for Comprehensive Reform

The whole is more than the sum of the parts: Experience from across the globe, including South Asia, indicates that although isolated measures to improve port performance have positive impacts, a comprehensive approach that tackles several interrelated angles yields greater benefits. South Asian governments should thus adopt a wide-ranging approach that tackles several interrelated angles rather than effect isolated measures. The approach should strengthen governance of the port sector, allow the private sector to take responsibilities and risks it is better suited to deal with than the public sector, and foster competition where feasible.

Strong governance and capacity of port authorities are requisites for the successful implementation of the landlord port model. Moving from a public sector monopoly to an unregulated private sector monopoly will not bring efficiency gains. Increases in private sector participation must go hand in hand with increased competition for and in the market. Where competition in the market is limited by substantial economies of scale, efficiency gains should come through adequate regulation.

### Notes

1. The absence of established international terminal operators differentiates Bangladesh from its subcontinent neighbors.

2. These berths do not have specialized containerized handling equipment and rely on geared vessels.

3. The Queen Elizabeth Quay was transferred to a private consortium on build, own, operate, and transfer (BOOT) concession, to be transferred back to the government after 40 years. The $240 million investment was partly financed by the Asian Development Bank, the International Finance Corporation, and the Commonwealth Development Corporation. The project constituted the first transportation PPP project in the country.

4. The first traffic arrived in 2012, but the port is not yet finished.

5. The only condition imposed that was eventually adopted was international competitive bidding for two of the South Harbor's three terminals. There has been only modest progress in reducing staff levels at SLPA, which were 10 times as high as at the much larger Port of Rotterdam at the time.

6. For the analysis, a port was considered a landlord port if it had implemented the model for at least six years during the 2000–10 period.

7. See Chlomoudis and Pallis (1998); Defilippi (2004); De Langen (2002); De Langen and Pallis (2006); Ferreira da Silva, Duarte, and Henrique Rocha (2012); Fleming and Baird (1999); Goss (1999); Haralambides (2002); Hoyle and Charlier (1995); Meersman and van de Voorde (2013); Slack (1985); Song (2002, 2003); Verhoeff (1981); Wan, Zhang, and Yuen (2013); Wan and Zhang (2013); Yap and Lam (2006); and Yuen, Zhang and Cheung (2013), among many others.

8. See Cullinane, Ji, and Wang (2005); Ishii and others (2013); Jacobs and Notteboom (2011); Kleywegt and others (2002); Lam and Yap (2011); Lee, Song, and Ducruet (2008); Low, Lam, and Tang (2009); Ryoo and Thanopoulou (1999); Slack and Wang (2002); Wang (1998); Yap and Lam (2006); and Yap and Notteboom (2011).

9. Transshipment traffic faces stronger competition than domestic traffic, because transshipment can take place almost anywhere along a maritime route.

10. This definition is from the ruling by the Court of Justice of the European Communities in *Hoffmann-La Roche & Co. AG v. Commission of the European Communities*, Case 85/76.

11. Visakhapatnam is the second-closest port to Kolkata (576 nautical miles away). Its container traffic volume is less than half that of Kolkata. The closest port, Paradip (179 nautical miles away), handles annual volume of just 9,000 TEUs.

12. In October 2012 an ICTSI subsidiary completed the acquisition of 35 percent of PICT, subsequently increasing its stake to 64.5 percent.

13. CMA and APSEZ formed a joint venture to operate the fourth container terminal at Mundra. When completed, in mid-2016, it will have annual capacity of 1.3 million TEUs.

## References

Andrés, L., J. L. Guasch, and S. López Azumendi. 2011. "Governance in State-Owned Enterprises Revisited: The Cases of Water and Electricity in Latin America and the Caribbean." World Bank Policy Research Working Paper Series, Washington, DC.

Chlomoudis, C. I., and A. A. Pallis. 1999. "Ports, Flexible Specialization, and Employment Patterns." Paper presented at the Eight World Conference on Transport Research, Antwerp, Belgium July 12–16, 1998.

Cullinane, K. P. B., P. Ji, and T. Wang. 2005. "The Relationship between Privatization and DEA Estimates of Efficiency in the Container Port Industry." *Journal of Economics and Business* 57 (5): 433–62.

Cullinane, K., and D. W. Song. 2003. "A Stochastic Frontier Model of the Productive Efficiency of Korean Container Terminals." *Applied Economics* 35 (3): 251–67.

Cullinane, K., D. W. Song, and R. Gray. 2002. "A Stochastic Frontier Model of the Efficiency of Major Container Terminals in Asia: Assessing the Influence of Administrative and Ownership Structures." *Transportation Research Part A: Policy and Practice* 36 (8): 743–62.

Defilippi, E. 2004. "Intra-port Competition, Regulatory Challenges and the Concession of Callao Port." *Maritime Economics and Logistics* 6 (4): 279–93.

De Langen, P. W. 2002. "Clustering and Performance: The Case of Maritime Clustering in the Netherlands." *Maritime Policy and Management* 29 (3): 209–21.

De Langen, P. W., and A. A. Pallis. 2006. "Analysis of the Benefits of Intra-port Competition." *International Journal of Transport Economics* 33 (1): 69–85.

Ducruet, C., and T. Notteboom. 2012. "The Worldwide Maritime Network of Container Shipping: Spatial Structure and Regional Dynamics." *Global Networks* 12 (3): 395–423.

Ferreira Da Silva, F., J. K. Duarte, and C. Henrique Rocha. 2012. "An Analysis of Demand Behavior in Brazilian Ports by Different Institutional or Natural Interventions." Social Science Research Network. http://papers.ssrn.com/sol3/papers.cfm?abstract_id =2186422.

Fiszbein, A., D. Ringold, and F. H. Rogers. 2011. "Making Services Work: Indicators, Assessments, and Benchmarking of the Quality and Governance of Public Service Delivery in the Human Development Sectors." World Bank Policy Research Working Paper, Washington, DC.

Fleming, D. K., and A. J. Baird. 1999. "Some Reflections on Port Competition in the United States and Western Europe." *Maritime Policy and Management* 26 (4): 383–94.

García, L. Y., and R. Sánchez. 2006. "Estadios de la competencia interportuaria: Del Marco institucional a la conducta estratégica." Paper presented at the Eighth World Economy Meeting, University of Oviedo, Spain. April 20–22.

Goss, R. O. 1999. "On the Distribution of Economic Rent in Seaports." *International Journal of Maritime Economics* 1 (1): 1–9.

Hall, P. V., and W. Jacobs. 2010. "Shifting Proximities: The Maritime Ports Sector in an Era of Global Supply Chains." *Regional Studies* 44 (9): 1103–15.

Haralambides, H. E. 2002. "Competition, Excess Capacity, and the Pricing of Port Infrastructure." *International Journal of Maritime Economics* 4 (4): 323–47.

Hoyle, B., and J. Charlier. 1995. "Inter-port Competition in Developing Countries: An East African Case Study." *Journal of Transport Geography* 3 (2): 87–103.

Ishii, M., P. T. W. Lee, K. Tezuka, and Y. T. Chang. 2013. "A Game Theoretical Analysis of Port Competition." *Transportation Research Part E: Logistics and Transportation Review* 49 (1): 92–106.

Jacobs, W., and T. Notteboom. 2011. "An Evolutionary Perspective on Regional Port Systems: The Role of Windows of Opportunity in Shaping Seaport Competition." *Environment and Planning A* 43 (7): 1674–92.

JLARC (Joint Legislative Audit and Review Commission). 2013. *Report to the Governor and the General Assembly of Virginia. Review of the Virginia Port Authority's Competitiveness, Funding and Governance.* House Document 17. Commonwealth of Virginia, Richmond.

Juang, Y. C., and M. Roe. 2010. "A Study on Success Factors of Development Strategies for Intermodal Freight Transport Systems." *Journal of the Eastern Asia Society for Transportation Studies* 8: 722–32.

Kleywegt, A. T., M. L. Goh, G. Y. Wu, and H. W. Zhang. 2002. *Competition between the Ports of Singapore and Malaysia.* Logistics Institute, Georgia Institute of Technology, and Logistics Institute-Asia Pacific, National University of Singapore.

Lam, J. S. L., and W. Y. Yap. 2011. "Container Port Competition and Complementarity in Supply Chain Systems: Evidence from the Pearl River Delta." *Maritime Economics and Logistics* 13 (2): 102–20.

Lee, S. W., D. W. Song, and C. Ducruet. 2008. "A Tale of Asia's World Ports: The Spatial Evolution in Global Hub Port Cities." *Geoforum* 39 (1): 372–85.

Limao, N., and A. J. Venables. 2001. "Infrastructure, Geographical Disadvantage, Transport Costs, and Trade." *World Bank Economic Review* 15 (3): 451–79

Lloyd's List. n.d. http://www.lloydslist.com/ll/sid/place/article51081.ece.

Low, J. M., S. W. Lam, and L. C. Tang. 2009. "Assessment of Hub Status among Asian Ports from a Network Perspective." *Transportation Research Part A: Policy and Practice* 43 (6): 593–606.

Meersman, H., and E. van de Voorde. 2013. "The Relationship between Economic Activity and Freight Transport." *Freight Transport Modelling* 7. Bingley (Emerald): 17–43.

Ministry of Road Transport and Highways. 2011. *Basic Port Statistics of India.* Transport Research Wing, Government of India, New Delhi.

———. 2013. *Basic Port Statistics of India.* Transport Research Wing, Government of India, New Delhi.

———. 2014. *Basic Port Statistics of India.* Transport Research Wing, Government of India, New Delhi.

Ministry of Shipping of India. 2014. Ministry of Shipping Annual Report. http://shipping.nic.in/index.php.

National Transport Development Policy Committee of India. 2014. "Our Approach to Transport Policy." Government of India, New Delhi. http://planningcommission.nic.in/reports/genrep/present_ntdpc2802.pdf.

Notteboom, T. E. 2002. "Consolidation and Contestability in the European Container Handling Industry." *Maritime Policy and Management* 29 (3): 257–69.

Notteboom, T., C. Coeck, and J. van den Broeck. 2000. "Measuring and Explaining the Relative Efficiency of Container Terminals by Means of Bayesian Stochastic Frontier Models." *International Journal of Maritime Economics* 2 (2): 83–106.

Notteboom T., F. Parola, and G. Satta. 2014. "State of the European Port System: Market Trends and Structure Update." *Partim Transshipment Volumes.*

Notteboom, T. E., and W. Winkelmans. 2001. "Structural Changes in Logistics: How Will Port Authorities Face the Challenge?" *Maritime Policy and Management* 28 (1): 71–89.

OECD (Organisation for Economic Co-operation and Development). 2011. *Competition in Ports and Port Services.* Document JT03313551, Directorate for Financial and Enterprise Affairs Competition Committee, Paris.

Port Finance India and Ernst & Young. 2012. *New Innings for the Indian Ports Sector.* http://www.portfinanceinternational.com/newsletter/2012india/special/PFI_India2012_Ernst&Young_report.pdf.

Raghuram, G., and Niraja Shukla. 2014. "Issues in PPPs in Ports in India." Working Paper 2014-01-06, Indian Institute of Management, Ahmedabad. http://www.iimahd.ernet.in/assets/snippets/workingpaperpdf/15518989842014-01-06.pdf.

Rodrigue, J. P. 2013. *The Geography of Transport Systems.* 3rd ed. New York: Routledge.

Rodrigue, J. P., and T. Notteboom. 2010. "Foreland-Based Regionalization: Integrating Intermediate Hubs with Port Hinterlands." *Research in Transportation Economics* 27 (1): 19–29.

Roy, D., and R. D. Koster. 2012. "Optimal Design of Container Terminal Layout." In *Proceedings of 12th International Material Handling Research Colloquium*, Gardanne, France.

Ryoo, D. K., and H. A. Thanopoulou. 1999. "Liner Alliances in the Globalization Era: A Strategic Tool for Asian Container Carriers." *Maritime Policy and Management* 26 (4): 349–67.

Saundry, R., and P. Turnbull. 1997. "Private Profit, Public Loss: The Financial and Economic Performance of UK Ports." *Maritime Policy and Management* 24 (4): 319–34.

Slack, B. 1985. "Containerization, Inter-port Competition and Port Selection." *Maritime Policy and Management* 12 (4): 293–303.

Slack, B., and A. Frémont. 2009. "Fifty Years of Organisational Change in Container Shipping: Regional Shift and the Role of Family Firms." *Geojournal* 74 (1): 23–34.

Slack, B., and, J. J. Wang. 2002. "The Challenge of Peripheral Ports: An Asian Perspective." *Geojournal* 56 (2): 159–66.

Song, D. W. 2002. "Regional Container Port Competition and Co-operation: The Case of Hong Kong and South China." *Journal of Transport Geography* 10 (2): 99–110.

———. 2003. "Port Competition in Concept and Practice." *Maritime Policy and Management* 30 (1): 29–44.

Sys, C. 2009. "Is the Container Liner Shipping Industry an Oligopoly?" *Transport Policy* 16 (5): 259–70.

Tull, M., and J. Reveley. 2001. "The Merits of Public versus Private Ownership: A Comparative Study of Australian and New Zealand Seaports." *Economic Papers: A Journal of Applied Economics and Policy* 20 (3): 75–99.

Verhoeff, J. M. 1981. "Seaport Competition: Some Fundamental and Political Aspects." *Maritime Policy and Management* 8 (1): 49–60.

Wan, Y., and A. Zhang. 2013. "Urban Road Congestion and Seaport Competition." *Journal of Transport Economics and Policy* 47(1): 55–70.

Wan, Y., A. Zhang, and A. C. Yuen. 2013. "Urban Road Congestion, Capacity Expansion and Port Competition: Empirical Analysis of US Container Ports." *Maritime Policy and Management* 40 (5): 417–38.

Wang, J. J. 1998. "A Container Load Center with a Developing Hinterland: A Case Study of Hong Kong." *Journal of Transport Geography* 6 (3): 187–201.

Wilmsmeier, G., and T. Notteboom. 2011. "Determinants of Liner Shipping Network Configuration: A Two-Region Comparison." *Geojournal* 76 (3): 213–28.

Wilson J. S., and T. Otsuki. 2007. "Regional Integration in South Asia: What Role for Trade Facilitation?" World Bank Policy Research Working Paper 4423, Washington, DC.

Yap, W. Y., and J. S. Lam. 2006. "Competition Dynamics between Container Ports in East Asia." *Transportation Research Part A: Policy and Practice* 40 (1): 35–51.

Yap, W. Y., and T. Notteboom. 2011. "Dynamics of Liner Shipping Service Scheduling and Their Impact on Container Port Competition." *Maritime Policy and Management* 38 (5): 471–85.

Yuen, A.C.L., Zhang, A. and Cheung, W., 2013. Foreign participation and competition: A way to improve the container port efficiency in China?. *Transportation Research Part A: Policy and Practice*, 49, pp. 220–231.

# CHAPTER 4

# Gains to Improved Port Performance in South Asia

## Introduction

Trade in South Asia almost doubled in the past decade, but it is still lower than other regions. Between 2000 and 2014, the region enjoyed the second-highest average annual economic growth in the world (6.8 percent), second only to East Asia (8.6 percent) (World Development Indicators Database). Trade in South Asia also experienced impressive growth, with trade as a share of GDP increasing by 18 percentage points between 2000 and 2014, compared with a 4 percentage points decline in East Asia.[1]

This progress notwithstanding, South Asia has a long way to go. In 2014 trade in South Asia represented just 47 percent of GDP, a smaller share than the 55 percent of East Asia. Moreover, the region relies almost exclusively on sea transport for its trade with the rest of the world. About 75 percent of South Asia's trade by value is transported by sea,[2] slightly higher than the world average of 70 percent (Rodrigue 2012).[3] Even some intraregional trade in South Asia goes by sea.[4]

Despite improvements over the past several years, South Asia continues to lag other regions in terms of competitiveness. Countries in the region still lack the institutional, business, and investment environments as well as the infrastructure needed to compete in the global economy. The most recent *Global Competitiveness Report* indicates that of all South Asia countries, only India and Sri Lanka score above the global average on competitiveness. Inadequate supply of infrastructure ranks among the top 4 most problematic factors for doing business in all South Asian countries other than Sri Lanka, where it ranks 10th.[5]

Transport and logistics are part of the reason for South Asia's low level of competitiveness. For transport infrastructure, South Asia performs below both the global average and the average for developing countries in Asia (WEF 2015). According to *Doing Business*, the cost of exporting or importing a container in South Asia is more than twice the cost in East Asia.[6] On average in South Asian countries, it takes 33 days to export and 34 days to import, effectively eliminating the time and cost advantages South Asia would have over East Asia on seaborne shipments to Europe and the East Coast of the United States.[7] South Asia also lags East Asia and the average middle-income country in overall logistics performance and logistics infrastructure, according to the 2014 Logistics Performance Index (http://lpi.worldbank.org/).[8]

A critical component of global competitiveness is the ability to move goods in and out of the region in a timely and cost-effective way. The link between transport and logistics costs and trade is clear: Better logistics performance leads to more trade, export diversification, attractiveness to foreign direct investment, and economic growth (Arvis and others 2012).[9] The region's ports are a critical link in the logistics chain that enables South Asian businesses to find overseas markets for their goods and to access competitively priced, high-quality imported goods. How ports operate has an impact on the time, cost, and efficiency of the entire logistics chain along domestic and regional freight corridors. The effects of port performance thus extend well beyond the coastline, affecting the competitiveness of businesses in the hinterland as well as in the region's landlocked nations. The performance of port operations has a direct impact on the cost of freight maritime transport and hence on global competitiveness and trade.

This chapter estimates the gains from improved port performance. The first section discusses drivers of maritime transport costs. The second presents the methodology and data used to assess whether improvements in port efficiency could reduce maritime transport costs. The last section provides some concluding remarks.

## Drivers of Maritime Transport Cost

Freight rates are volatile and sensitive to movements in the economy. As the global economy grew in 2000–08, demand for container shipping increased at an annual average growth rate of about 10 percent (UNCTAD 2014). The supply of containerized cargo grew at a slightly higher rate. These demand and supply factors are some of the determinants of maritime costs; others include distance to trade partner, competition, quality of infrastructure, and port efficiency.

### Distance and Oil

Distance is historically one of the main variables used in analyzing barriers to trade. Transport costs are proportional to distance, albeit in a complex fashion, and higher costs reduce trade.

Two main types of direct costs are associated with distance: time and fuel. Shipping operators require labor inputs, for which the marginal cost (wages) is proportional to the time spent at sea. Longer times on ocean legs are associated with losses in productivity, as the same ship would be able to haul more merchandise over shorter distances. Technological advances lead to an increase in the size of ships and a decrease in the overall time ships spend at sea. Bigger and faster ships allow more merchandise to be carried at lower cost. However, larger ships take more time at docks to unload, implying an inverse relationship between costs and size (OECD 2008). Fuel costs are also higher for longer distances. They rose steadily after 2000, peaking in 2008. An unintended consequence of rising fuel costs was that ship operators tended to reduce vessel speeds to compensate for higher prices, reducing productivity. There is thus a feedback effect between time and fuel costs.

### Trade Imbalances

Trade asymmetries have a large and significant effect on trade costs. Greece, for example, imports 60 percent more than it exports, while Ireland exports 40 percent more than it imports (Baldwin and Taglioni 2006). If the majority of trade occurs in one country (country 1 exports to country 2 while importing nothing from country 2), ships may haul empty containers on one leg of the journey and return with full containers. The exporter who receives the empty containers and sends the containers back packed often bears a higher cost. For example, India has a favorable trade balance with the United States. In the first half of 2008, hauling a container from the United States to India cost about $1,500, while hauling it in the opposite direction cost about $2,500 (Korinek and Sourdin 2009). Directional trade imbalances serve as a proxy for ships that carry empty containers on one leg of the journey (Clark, Dollar, and Micco 2004).

### Trade Volume and Value

The volume of freight is used to capture economies of scale. Higher demand for goods (that is, an increase in the volume of trade) is associated with lower costs. The value of shipped goods does not always factor in the cost of shipping when costs are based on containers and weight equivalents. In practice, however, liner shipping companies distinguish between different types of goods and may charge higher insurance premiums for high-value goods, which correlates the value of goods and transport costs (Wilmsmeier, Hoffmann, and Sánchez 2006). The insurance component can represent up to 15 percent of total transport costs (Clark, Dollar, and Micco 2004).

### Containerization

A large share of goods traded is shipped in containers, as opposed to tankers and dry bulk. Containerization should reduce transport costs, because containers are easy to load and unload, and result in a larger volume of goods shipped.

A number of empirical studies, however, suggest that ocean transportation costs did not decrease much as a consequence of containerization (Bridgman 2014; Hummels 2007; Sánchez and others 2003). One possible explanation is that transportation is not a conventionally competitive market, that cargo companies are able to exercise market power through legal cartels (Hummels, Lugovskyy, and Skiba 2009). For this reason, innovations and freight rates do not necessarily have a one-for-one relationship (Bridgman 2014).

Another possible explanation is that monetary costs do not fully capture the real gains from containerization, which might come from quality changes in transportation services, such as faster ships and quicker loading and unloading than with break bulk (Hummels 2007). The marginal gains from further containerization seem to be small if containerization is already high. The technological effects associated with containerization are thus once-off effects.

### Competition

Mark-ups in the shipping industry take many forms. They often fall when rival companies compete on trade routes. In contrast, on low-volume routes, shippers often operate as monopolies or cartels. Mark-ups on these routes are higher, as a result of price-fixing or cooperation agreements among shipping lines.

Cargo reservation schemes still exist under the UN Liner Code, but regulation has reduced the extent of anticompetitive practices such as price-fixing agreements and maritime conferences.[10] Other forms of protection, such as barriers to investment in maritime transport service, still exist (one example is the limitations foreign investors face when establishing local offices). Bertho, Bochert, and Mattoo (2014) find that policy barriers reduce trade by 28–46 percent through higher transport costs.

### Infrastructure and Efficiency

Efficient ports have shorter turnaround (loading and unloading) times and lower handling costs. In some cases port efficiency is the most important determinant of transportation costs: Doubling port efficiency reduces costs by as much as halving the distance between countries (Wilmsmeier, Hoffmann, and Sánchez 2006). Efficient ports reduce maritime transport costs: A 0.1 increase in port efficiency decreases maritime transport costs by 0.9–3.8 percent (Blonigen and Wilson 2008; Clark, Dollar, and Micco 2004; Micco and Perez 2002; Wilmsmeier, Hoffmann, and Sánchez 2006).

The literature on maritime transport costs has struggled to identify a consistent measure of port efficiency, often resorting to surveys; proxy variables, such as infrastructure development or GDP; and econometric techniques. A consistent efficiency measure would capture changes in port enhancements while keeping track of competing ports. Detailed input information across ports and over time is thus required to construct an adequate measure of port efficiency.

Table 4.1 summarizes some of the results from the literature. Although the studies use different datasets and methodologies, they find similar effects.

## Port Efficiency and Maritime Transport Costs

This section presents the methodology and data used to assess whether improvements in port performance across the Indian and Western Pacific Oceans could reduce maritime transport costs. Readers not interested in the technical aspects of the analysis should skip the first three subsections.

### Methodology

The econometric model used is based on Fink, Mattoo, and Neagu (2002). Maritime transport charges are assumed to be equal to the marginal cost

**Table 4.1 Factors Affecting Maritime Transport Costs: Summary of Regression Results from the Literature**

| Author/year | Period | Distance | Imbalance between imports and exports | Value-weight | Container | Weight | Volume | Efficiency |
|---|---|---|---|---|---|---|---|---|
| Blonigen and Wilson (2008) | 1991–2003 | 0.13*** 0.21*** | Imports (–0.00) Exports (–0.00) | 0.55*** | –0.04*** | 0.91*** | 0.00*** | –0.09, –0.06[a] |
| Fink and others (2002) | 1998 | 0.33*** | | | –0.07** | | –0.02** | |
| Micco and Perez (2002) | 1995–99 | 0.17*** | | 0.55*** | –0.02 | | –0.04*** | –0.07*** |
| Sánchez and others (2003) | 2002 | 0.09 | | 0.54*** | –0.02 | | | 0.03, –0.06, 0.00[b] |
| Limao and Venables (2001) | 1998 | 0.38** | | | | | | |
| Wilmsmeier, Hoffmann, and Sánchez (2006) | 2002 | 0.35*** | 0.00* | 0.34*** | | –0.09*** | –0.02**[c] | –0.38*** |
| Clark, Dollar, and Micco (2004) | 1998 | 0.18*** | –0.07*** | 0.55*** | –0.03** | | –0.04*** | –0.06*** |

*Notes:*
a. The first result compares the Port of Oakland with the most efficient port in the United States (Richmond-Petersburg), where port charges are about 9 percent lower. The second result compares the Port of Rotterdam with the most efficient port outside the United States in the sample considered by the authors (Zeebrugge, Belgium), where port charges are 6 percent lower.
b. The results are related to time inefficiency, productivity, and stay per vessel, respectively.
c. The result is for bilateral trade.
Significance level: * = 10 percent level, ** = 5 percent level, *** = 1 percent level.

multiplied by shipping companies' mark-up. Expressed in logarithm, the pricing formula becomes the sum of the marginal cost component and the mark-up component:

$$p_{ikt} = mc(i,k,t) + u(i,k,t) \qquad (4.1)$$

where $p_{ik}$ is the unit transport cost, in logarithm, for commodity $k$ transported between exporter country $i$ and the United States in year t, and $k$ is the commodity transported in containers only. The marginal cost term is expressed as

$$mc(i,k,t) = \alpha + \lambda_k + \beta_1 T_{ikt} + \beta_2 d_{it} + \beta_3 q_{it} + \beta_4 Imb_{it} +$$
$$\beta_5 VW_{ikt} + \beta_6 Y_t + \beta_7 PE_t \qquad (4.2)$$

where $\alpha$ captures importing country–specific effects, such as port services and auxiliary services (which are not part of the dependent variable). Differences in commodities shipped are specified by $\lambda_\kappa$. $T_{i\kappa}$ corresponds to the containerization variables (expressed as a share of all types of cargo). The logarithm of the product of oil prices and distance ($d_{it}$) is included to capture possible costs associated with distance, as it varies over time with regard to fuel consumption (as explained below, there are only 12 trade routes and as such very little variation in distance).

Economies of scale, $q_{it}$, measured as total weight of imports carried by liners, in logarithm, are expected to reduce costs. The trade imbalance measure, $Imb_{it}$, is assumed to capture the imbalance in container shipping between country $i$ and the United States.[11] $VW_{ikt}$ is the value per weight measure for commodity $k$, in logarithm. The logarithm of exporting country GDP per capita ($Y_{it}$) is included as a proxy for infrastructure development of the country. $PE_{it}$ is the efficiency variable.

Mark-ups, in logarithm, are expressed as

$$u(i,k,t) = u_k + \beta_8 CI_{it} \tag{4.3}$$

Product specific effects are captured by $u_\kappa$. $CI_{it}$, the liner shipping connectivity index, captures how well countries are connected to global shipping networks.[12] Substituting equations (4.2) and (4.3) into equation (4.1) yields the equation to be estimated:

$$p(i,k,t) = \alpha + \beta_k + \beta_1 T_{ikt} + \beta_2 d_{it} + \beta_3 q_{it} + \beta_4 Imb_{it} +$$
$$\beta_5 VW_{ikt} + \beta_6 Y_{it} + \beta_7 PE_{it} + \beta_8 CI_{it} + \varepsilon_{ikt} \tag{4.4}$$

where $\beta_\kappa = (\lambda_\kappa + u_\kappa)$ and $\varepsilon_{ikt}$ is assumed to be i.i.d.

The within-transformation is used to estimate equation (4.4). The fixed-effects model controls for commodity heterogeneity (that is, not all commodity costs share similar features). A set of trade-pair dummies are included to control for differences in country characteristics, and time dummies are included to control for time-specific events, thereby controlling for port-specific costs (average by country) over time.

### Data

The dataset was compiled from the OECD Maritime Transport Cost dataset, the UN Comtrade database, the World Bank's World Development Indicators, and sea-distances.org. The OECD Maritime Transport Cost dataset contains data at the country, not the port, level, and only for the period 2000–07. The analysis was conducted at the country level for exporting countries for which data on exports shipped to the United States in containers were available: Bangladesh, India, Pakistan, and Sri Lanka; Indonesia, Malaysia, the Philippines, and Vietnam; and Kenya, Mauritius, South Africa, and Tanzania. Figure 4.1 shows the importance of exports to the United States as a share of total exports from the countries considered in the analysis.

The OECD Maritime Transport Cost database includes actual transport costs (insurance and freight), unit transport costs (the cost to transport one kilogram of merchandise), and an ad valorem equivalent (the transport cost divided by the total import value). The data are disaggregated at the Harmonized System (HS) two-digit level.[13] Actual costs include the freight, insurance, and other charges (excluding import duties) of bringing merchandise alongside the carrier at the

**Figure 4.1  Exports to the United States by Selected Countries, 2007**

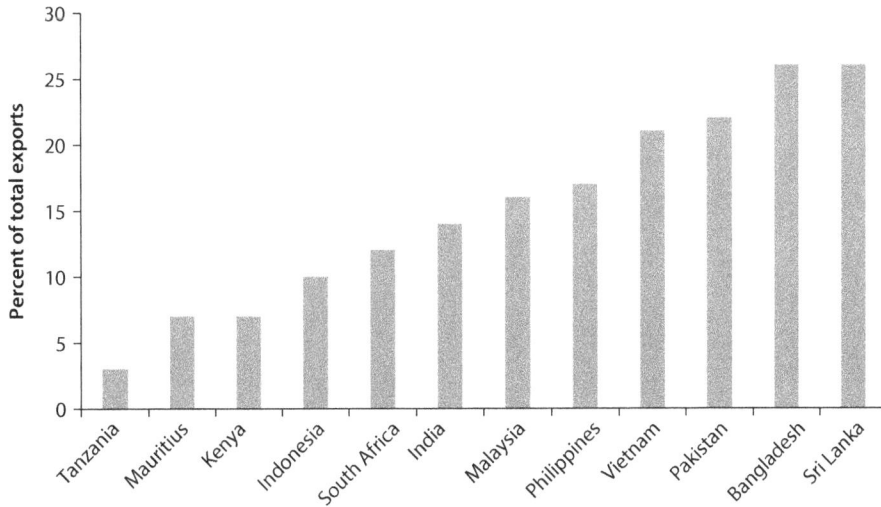

*Source:* UN Comtrade data.

origin port and placing it alongside the carrier at the first port of entry from the importing country (OECD 2008). Port charges are thus included. The weight of imports in kilograms (cost divided by unit cost) is calculated from the dataset.

Table 4.2 presents the descriptive statistics of the main variables used in the analysis.[14] The distance variable captures the overall distance liner ships cover to bring merchandise from the origin (main exporting country port) to the destination country (the Port of Baltimore, in the United States).[15] The efficiency measures are constructed from an intertemporal data envelopment analysis (DEA) assuming variable and constant returns to scale to capture pure and scale efficiency.

## Impact of Port Efficiency on Maritime Transport Costs and Trade

A variety of factors explain differences in maritime transport costs for exports from countries in the Indian and Western Pacific Oceans to the United States (table 4.3).[16] Products with higher value per kilogram cost more to transport, as do products that travel longer distances. The results of the analysis confirm the existence of economies of scale, as transport costs decrease with weight. The weight variable is a possible proxy for routes frequented by larger ships. It could also capture some effects of technological change; the ability of liners to carry more and heavier containers hints at innovation. Larger flows of exports to the United States relative to imports from the United States (that is, lower directional trade imbalances) means that empty containers come to the country to pick up exports, raising maritime transport costs. A 10 percent decrease in the trade imbalance increases maritime transport costs by about 2 percent. Exporting countries with higher GDP per capita face lower maritime transport costs for their exports, potentially as a consequence of better trade infrastructure and services.[17]

**Table 4.2 Descriptive Statistics of Main Variables Used in the Analysis**

| Variable | Mean | Standard deviation | Minimum | Maximum |
|---|---|---|---|---|
| Unit cost (ln) | −1.30 | 0.94 | −9.21 | 4.95 |
| Ad valorem | 0.09 | 0.06 | 0.00 | 0.71 |
| Value-weight (ln) | 1.38 | 1.09 | −2.82 | 7.83 |
| Weight (ln) | 12.93 | 3.43 | 1.39 | 20.57 |
| Imbalance | −0.44 | 0.31 | −0.85 | 0.66 |
| Oil*Distance (ln) | 12.81 | 0.44 | 12.04 | 13.61 |
| Efficiency (variable returns to scale) | 0.45 | 0.17 | 0.10 | 1.00 |
| Connectivity | 26.33 | 16.92 | 5.07 | 81.58 |
| Containerization | 0.63 | 0.28 | 0.16 | 1.00 |
| GDP per capita (ln) | 7.06 | 0.86 | 5.72 | 8.88 |

Note: Sample summary statistics exclude omitted data.

**Table 4.3 Determinants of Maritime Transport Costs**

| | Dependent variable: Unit transport cost (ln) | | |
|---|---|---|---|
| Variable | (1) | (2) | (3) |
| Oil prices*distance (ln) | 0.02 (0.02) | 0.10** (0.04) | 0.10** (0.04) |
| Value-weight (ln) | 0.60*** (0.03) | 0.60*** (0.03) | 0.60*** (0.03) |
| Containerization (percent) | 0.19 (0.13) | 0.24* (0.13) | 0.25* (0.13) |
| Directional imbalance (percent) | −0.17* (0.09) | −0.22** (0.10) | −0.21** (0.10) |
| Weight (ln) | −0.07*** (0.01) | −0.07*** (0.01) | −0.07*** (0.01) |
| *Policy variables* | | | |
| Port efficiency | −0.22*** (0.08) | −0.24*** (0.08) | −0.23*** (0.07) |
| GDP per capita (ln) | | −0.17** (0.07) | −0.17** (0.07) |
| Connectivity index | | | −0.19 (0.29) |
| $R^2$ | 0.26 | 0.26 | 0.26 |
| F-statistic | 362.94 | 312.20 | 273.18 |

Note: White standard errors are in parentheses, as Wooldridge's serial correlation test for short fixed-effects panels could not reject the null hypothesis of no serial autocorrelation. Number of observations was 5,906.
Significance level: * = 10 percent level, ** = 5 percent level, *** = 1 percent level.

Countries with more efficient port sectors incur lower maritime transport costs in their exports to the United States: Both the measure capturing pure efficiency in the use of port facilities and the measure capturing pure and scale efficiency are significant under all specifications. No difference is evident between the two measures of efficiency, which are highly correlated (0.87), as pure efficiency is the main driver. Hence only results for pure efficiency are reported and discussed.

Efficiency scores range from 0 (most inefficient) to 1 (most efficient). A 0.1 increase in the average pure efficiency score for the port sector in a country reduces the maritime transport cost of its exports to the United States by about 2.3 percent. Moving from the bottom efficiency 25th percentile to the top one reduces transport costs by about 2.9 percent. Thus if Vietnam improved its port efficiency to the levels of the Philippines, its maritime transport costs would fall by about 2.9 percent on average.

On average, maritime transport costs in Bangladesh, India, and Pakistan would have been 0.6–8.8 percent lower during 2000–07 if their port sectors had been as efficient as the port sector in Sri Lanka, the country in the sample with the most efficient port sector over this period (figure 4.2). If the port sectors of all the countries in the Indian and Western Pacific Oceans analyzed had been as efficient as the port sector of Sri Lanka during 2000–07, their maritime transport costs would have been about 8.5 percent lower, on average.

If the port sectors of Bangladesh, India, and Pakistan had been as efficient as the port sector of Sri Lanka, the average value of their exports to the United States would have been 0.5–7.0 percent higher. Using the same dataset, Korinek and Sourdin (2009) estimate that a 10 percent reduction in maritime transport costs increases trade by about 8 percent. Using their estimate together with the estimated effect of port efficiency from figure 4.2 yields potential average gains from efficiency improvements of 0.5 percent for Bangladesh, 7.0 percent for India and Pakistan, and 6.8 percent for the sample as a whole.

**Figure 4.2  Average Cost Reduction Associated with Becoming as Efficient as the Most Efficient Country, 2000–07**

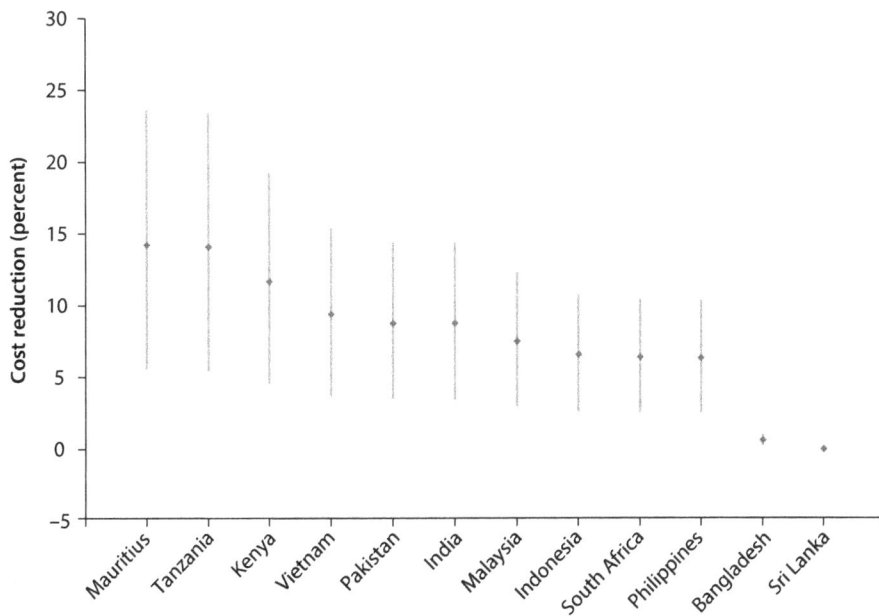

*Note:* Bar width represents 95 percent standard errors.

## Concluding Remarks

Trade in South Asia almost doubled between 2000 and 2014, rising from 29 percent to 47 percent of GDP. It relies almost exclusively on sea transport, with about 75 percent of trade by value moving through ports. The analysis in this chapter shows that governments interested in increasing the competitiveness of their exports need to focus on improving the performance of their port sector.

On average, the efficiency with which container ports in South Asia used their facilities rose over the period studied. Some countries and ports still have a long way to go to catch up to the best-performing container ports in the Indian and Western Pacific Oceans, however. If the port sectors of Bangladesh, India, and Pakistan had been as efficient as the port sector of Sri Lanka, the average value of their exports to the United States would have been 0.5–7.0 percent higher. The potential gains associated with improving port performance in South Asia are thus huge.

## Notes

1. Between 2000 and 2014, exports as a share of GDP increased by 8 percentage points in South Asia and decreased by 2 percentage points in East Asia.
2. In 2012, 78 percent of South Asia's trade by value was with countries in Asia-Pacific Economic Cooperation (APEC) or the European Union.
3. In terms of kilograms per kilometer traveled, about 99 percent of South Asia's trade is transported by sea; the world average is 95 percent (Cristea and others 2013).
4. The Port of Colombo is the region's primary container port. It serves as a transshipment hub for goods moving around the region. A large share of the trade between India and Pakistan and between Bangladesh and Pakistan is by sea. Much of the trade between Pakistan and India is transshipped through the Port of Dubai.
5. It is first in Bangladesh and Pakistan, third in Nepal, and fourth in Bhutan and India. Afghanistan and Maldives are not included in the report.
6. If only coastal countries are considered in both regions, the cost of a container with exports is 46 percent higher in South Asia than in East Asia, and the cost of a container with imports is 59 percent higher (Doing Business database 2014).
7. The average for East Asia is 20 days for exports and 22 days for imports. For coastal countries only, the difference between South Asia and East Asia narrow to only two days for both exports and imports (Doing Business database 2014).
8. South Asian countries also rank low in terms of global connectivity. The Liner Shipping Connectivity Index, which captures how well countries are connected to global shipping networks, is 165 for China, 54 for Sri Lanka, and 45 for India.
9. According to Behar and Venables (2011), in an average-size developing country, a one standard deviation improvement in logistics performance would raise exports by about 36 percent, the equivalent of a 14 percent reduction in the distance between two trade partners. Djankov, Freund, and Pham (2010) find that a one-day transit delay caused by inefficiencies in the logistics chain reduces the volume of trade by 1 percent.
10. Competition laws such as the United States' Ocean Shipping Reform Act of 1999, European regulation that abolished block exemptions from shipping conferences,

and the emergence of large ship owners in the 1980s and 1990s weakened conferences (WTO 2010).

11. The trade imbalance is calculated as total U.S. exports to the destination country minus imports from that country as a ratio of total trade between the two countries.

12. The liner shipping connectivity index is based on five components: the number of ships, their container-carrying capacity, the maximum vessel size, the number of services, and the number of countries that deploy container ships in a country's port. The country with the highest average in 2004 has an index of 100.

13. The Harmonized System is an international nomenclature for the classification of products developed by the United Nations. It allows participating countries to classify traded goods on a common basis for customs purposes. At the international level, a six-digit code system is used, in which the first two digits identify the chapter the goods are classified in.

14. There are 5,906 observations after excluding censored observations and various outliers.

15. Baltimore was chosen so that the results here could be compared with those of other studies, such as Limao and Venables (2001). The Port of New York/New Jersey is the largest port on the East Coast. The distance between the two ports (about 200 miles) is marginal and identical for all countries; the results would therefore not change if New York/New Jersey had been used.

16. The estimates are fairly robust and consistent given multiple controls and specifications.

17. Containerization has no effect on transport costs, a result similar to Sanchez and others (2003), Bridgman (2014), and several other empirical studies. A possible explanation raised by Hummels (2007) is that "the real gains from containerization might come from unmeasured quality change in transportation services" such as faster ships as well as quicker loading and unloading than with break bulk.

## References

Arvis, J. F., M. A. Mustra, L. Ojala, B. Shepherd, and D. Saslavsky. 2012. *Connecting to Compete: Trade Logistics in the Global Economy*. Washington, DC: World Bank. http://www.worldbank.org/content/dam/Worldbank/document/Trade/LPI2014.pdf.

Baldwin, R., and D. Taglioni. 2006. "Gravity for Dummies and Dummies for Gravity Equations." NBER Working Paper 12516, National Bureau of Economic Research, Cambridge, MA.

Behar, A., and A. J. Venables. 2011. "Transport Costs and International Trade." In *A Handbook of Transport Economics*, edited by A. de Palma, R. Lindsey, E. Quinet, and R. Vickerman, 97–115. Northampton, MA: Edward Elgar.

Bertho, F., I. Bochert, and A. Mattoo. 2014. "The Trade-Reducing Effects of Restrictions on Liner Shipping." Policy Research Working Paper WPS6921, World Bank, Washington, DC.

Blonigen, B. A., and W. W. Wilson. 2008. "Port Efficiency and Trade Flows." *Review of International Economics* 16 (1): 21–36.

Bridgman, B. 2014. "Why Containerization Did Not Reduce Ocean Trade Shipping Cost." Bureau of Economic Analysis, U.S. Department of Labor, Washington, DC.

Clark, X., D. Dollar, and A. Micco. 2004. "Port Efficiency, Maritime Transport Costs, and Bilateral Trade." *Journal of Development Economics* 75 (2): 417–50.

Cristea, A., D. Hummels, L. Puzzello, and M. Avetisyan. 2013. "Trade and the Greenhouse Gas Emissions from International Freight Transport." *Journal of Environmental Economics and Management* 65 (1): 153–73.

Djankov, S., C. Freund, and C. S. Pham. 2010. "Trading on Time." *Review of Economics and Statistics* 92 (1): 166–73.

Doing Business Indicators (database). 2014. World Bank, Washington, DC. http://www .doingbusiness.org/data.

Fink, C., A. Mattoo, and I. C. Neagu. 2002. "Trade in International Maritime Services: How Much Does Policy Matter?" *World Bank Economic Review* 16 (1): 81–108.

Hummels, D. 2007. "Transportation Costs and International Trade in the Second Era of Globalization." *Journal of Economic Perspectives* 21 (3): 131–54.

Hummels, D., V. Lugovskyy, and A. Skiba. 2009. "The Trade Reducing Effects of Market Power in International Shipping." *Journal of Development Economics* 89 (1): 84–97.

Korinek, J., and P. Sourdin. 2009. "Maritime Transport Costs and Their Impact on Trade." https://eclass.unipi.gr/modules/document/file.php/NAS274/mar%20cost%20 %26%20trade.pdf.

Limao, N. and A. J. Venables. 2001. "Infrastructure, Geographical Disadvantage, Transport Costs and Trade." *World Bank Economic Review* 15 (3): 451–79.

Micco, A., and N. Pérez. 2002. "Determinants of Maritime Transport Costs." IADB Working Paper 441, Inter-American Development Bank, Washington, DC.

OECD (Organisation for Economic Co-operation and Development) 2008. *Clarifying Trade Costs in Maritime Transport*. Paris: TAD/TC/WP.

Rodrigue, J. P. 2012. "The Geography of Global Supply Chains: Evidence from Third-Party Logistics." *Journal of Supply Chain Management* 48 (3): 15–23.

Sánchez, R. J., J. Hoffmann, A. Micco, G. A. Pizzolitto, M. Sgut, and G. Wilmsmeier. 2003. "Port Efficiency and International Trade: Port Efficiency as a Determinant of Maritime Transport Costs." *Maritime Economics and Logistics* 5: 199–218.

UNCTAD (United Nations Conference on Trade and Development). 2008. *Review of Maritime Transport 2008*. Geneva: UNCTAD.

———. 2014. *Review of Maritime Transport 2014*. Geneva: UNCTAD.

WEF (World Economic Forum). 2015. *Global Competitiveness Report*. http://www .weforum.org/docs/wef_globalcompetitivenessreport_2014-15.pdf.

Wilmsmeier, G., J. Hoffmann, and R. Sánchez. 2006. "The Impact of Port Characteristics on International Maritime Transport Costs." *Port Economics: Research in Transportation Economics*, vol. 16, edited by K. Cullinane and W. Talley. Amsterdam: Elsevier.

World Bank. n.d. *Container Traffic*. Washington, DC: World Bank. http://data.worldbank .org/indicator/IS.SHP.GOOD.TU.

———. n.d. *Economy & Growth*. Washington, DC: World Bank. http://data.worldbank. org/topic/economy-and-growth.

WTO (World Trade Organization). 2010. "Maritime Transport Services." Background note by the Secretariat, S/C/W/315, WTO, Geneva.

# Studies of Port Efficiency and Productivity

**Table A.1 Recent Applications of Data Envelopment Analysis to Estimation of Container Port Efficiency**

| Author/year of study | Coverage | Period |
|---|---|---|
| Barros (2003, 2004) | Portuguese port industry | 1999–2000 |
| Barros (2006) | Italian ports | 2002–03 |
| Barros and Athanassiou (2004) | Portuguese and Greek seaports | 1998–2000 |
| Bichou (2011) | Container terminals | 2002–08 |
| Bonilla and others (2004) | Spanish port system | 1995–98 |
| Cullinane, Ji, and Wang (2005) | World's top 30 container ports | 2001 |
| Cullinane and Wang (2010) | 25 of world's top container ports in 2001 | 1992–99 |
| Estache, Tovar, and Trujillo (2004) | Mexico's main ports | 1996–99 |
| Hung, Lu, and Wang (2010) | Asian container ports | 2007 |
| Itoh (2002) | Japan's international container ports | 1990–99 |
| Li, Luan, and Pian (2013) | Coastal container terminals in China | |
| Liu (2008) | 10 Asian-Pacific ports | 1998–2001 |
| Lu and Wang (2013) | Major container terminals in China and the Republic of Korea | 2010 |
| Martínez-Budría and others (1999) | Spanish port authorities | 1993–97 |
| Mokhtar (2013) | Container terminals in peninsular Malaysia | 2003–10 |
| Park and De (2004) | Ports in the Republic of Korea | 1999 |
| Rios and Gastaud Maçada (2006) | Container terminals in Mercosur region | 2002–04 |
| Schoyen and Odeck (2013) | Norwegian container ports | 2002–08 |
| Suárez-Alemán, Trujillo, and Cullinane (2014) | African ports | 2010 |
| Tongzon (2001) | Australian and other international container ports | 1996 |
| Turner, Windle, and Dresner (2004) | North American ports | 1984–97 |
| Valentine and Gray (2001) | 31 of top 100 container ports | 1998 |
| Wang and Cullinane (2006) | European container terminals | 2003 |

*Source:* Updated from Suárez-Alemán, Trujillo, and Cullinane 2014.
*Note:* Cullinane and Wang (2010) provide a comprehensive review of some of these studies.

**Table A.2 Studies That Measure the Malmquist Index for Ports**

| Author/year of study | Region | Period |
|---|---|---|
| Al-Eraqi, Khader, and Mustafa (2009) | Middle East and East African container terminals | 2000–05 |
| Barros, Felício, and Fernandes (2012) | Brazilian seaports | 2004–10 |
| Bo-xin, Xiang-qun, and G. Zi-jian (2009) | Chinese container ports | 2001–06 |
| Chang and Tovar (2014) | Peruvian and Chilean ports | 2004–10 |
| Cheon, Dowall, and Song (2010) | Worldwide ports | 1991–94 |
| Choi (2011) | Chinese container ports | 2003–08 |
| Díaz Hernández, Martínez-Budría, and Jara-Díaz (2008) | Spanish ports | 1994–98 |
| Estache, Tovar, and Trujillo (2004) | Mexican industrial ports | 1996–99 |
| Guerrero and Rivera (2009) | Mexican ports | 2000–07 |
| Halkos and Tzeremes (2012) | Greek ports | 2006–10 |
| Haralambides and others (2010) | Middle East and East African ports | 2005–07 |
| Lozano (2009) | Spanish port authorities | 2002–06 |
| Martín Bofarull (2003) | Spanish ports | Theoretical |
| Mokhtar and Shah (2013) | Major container ports in peninsular Malaysia | 2003–10 |
| Song and Cui (2014) | Chinese container terminals | 2006–11 |
| Wilmsmeier, Tovar, and Sánchez (2013) | Latin America and the Caribbean and Spain | 2005–11 |

# References

Al-Eraqi, A., A. Khader, and A. Mustafa. 2009. "DEA Malmquist Index Measurement in Middle East and East African Containers Terminals." *International Journal of Shipping and Transport Logistics* 1 (3): 249–59.

Barros, C. P. 2003. "Incentive Regulation and Efficiency of Portuguese Port Authorities." *Maritime Economics and Logistics* 5 (1): 55–69.

———. 2004. "The Measurement of Efficiency of Portuguese Sea Port Authorities with DEA." *International Journal of Transport Economics* 30 (3): 335–54.

———. 2006. "A Benchmark Analysis of Italian Seaports Using Data Envelopment Analysis." *Maritime Economics and Logistics* 8 (4): 347–65.

Barros, C. P., and M. Athanassiou. 2004. "Efficiency in European Seaports with DEA: Evidence from Greece and Portugal." *Maritime Economics and Logistics* 6 (2): 122–40.

Barros, C. P., J. A. Felício, and R. L. Fernandes. 2012. "Productivity Analysis of Brazilian Seaports." *Maritime Policy and Management* 39 (5): 503–23.

Bichou, K. 2011. "A Two-Stage Supply Chain DEA Model for Measuring Container/Terminal Efficiency." *International Journal of Shipping and Transport Logistics* 3 (1): 6–26.

Bonilla, M., T. Casasus, A. Medal, and R. Sala. 2004. "An Efficiency Analysis of the Spanish Port System." *International Journal of Transport Economics* 31 (3): 379–400.

Bo-xin, F., S. Xiang-qun, and G. Zi-jian. 2009. "DEA-Based Malmquist Productivity Index Measure of Operating Efficiencies: New Insights with an Application to Container Ports." *Journal Shanghai Jiaotong University* 14 (4): 490–96.

Chang, V., and B. Tovar. 2014. "Efficiency and Productivity Changes for Peruvian and Chilean Ports Terminals: A Parametric Distance Functions Approach." *Transport Policy* 31 (C): 83–94.

Cheon, S., D. Dowall, and D. W. Song. 2010. "Evaluating Impacts of Institutional Reforms on Port Efficiency Changes: Ownership, Corporate Structure, and Total Factor Productivity Changes of World Container Ports." *Transport Research (Part E): Logistics and Transportation Review*: 46 (4) 546–61.

Choi, Y. 2011. "The Efficiency of Major Ports under Logistics Risk in Northeast Asia." *Asia-Pacific Journal of Operational Research* 28 (1): 111–23.

Cullinane, K. P. B., P. Ji, and T. Wang. 2005. "The Relationship between Privatization and DEA Estimates of Efficiency in the Container Port Industry." *Journal of Economics and Business* 57 (5): 433–62.

Cullinane, K. P. B., and T. Wang. 2010. "The Efficiency Analysis of Container Port Production Using DEA Panel Data Approaches." *OR Spectrum* 32 (3): 717–38.

Díaz -Hernández, J. J., E. Martínez-Budría, and S. Jara-Díaz. 2008. "Productivity in Cargo Handling in Spanish Ports during a Period of Regulatory Reforms." *Networks and Spatial Economics* 8 (2–3): 287–95.

Estache, A., B. Tovar, and L. Trujillo. 2004. "Sources of Efficiency Gains in Port Reform: A DEA Decomposition of a Malmquist TFP Index for Mexico." *Utilities Policy* 12 (4): 221–30.

Guerrero, C., and C. Rivera. 2009. "Mexico: Total Productivity Changes at the Principal Container Ports." *CEPAL Review* 99 (December): 173–85.

Halkos, G., and N. Tzeremes. 2012. "Measuring Seaports' Productivity: A Malmquist Productivity Index Decomposition Approach." MRPA 40174, University of Munich.

Haralambides, H., M. Hussain, C. P. Barros, and N. Peypoch. 2010. "A New Approach and Benchmarking Seaport Efficiency and Technological Change." *International Journal of Transport Economics* 37 (1): 77–96.

Hung, S.-H., W. M. Lu, and T. P. Wang. 2010. "Benchmarking the Operating Efficiency of Asia Container Ports." *European Journal of Operational Research* 203 (3): 706–13.

Itoh, H. 2002. "Efficiency Changes at Major Container Ports in Japan: A Window Application of Data Envelopment Analysis." *Review of Urban and Regional Development Studies* 14 (2): 133–52.

Li, D., W. Luan, and F. Pian. 2013. "The Efficiency Measurement of Coastal Container Terminals in China." *Journal of Transportation Systems Engineering and Information Technology* 13 (5): 10–15.

Liu, C.-C. 2008. "Evaluating the Operational Efficiency of Major Ports in the Asia-Pacific Region Using Data Envelopment Analysis." *Applied Economics* 40 (13): 1737–43.

Lozano, S. 2009. "Estimating Productivity Growth of Spanish Ports Using a Non-radial, Non-oriented Malmquist Index." *International Journal of Shipping and Transport Logistics* 1 (3): 227–48.

Lu, B., and X. Wang. 2013. "A Comparative Study on Increasing Efficiency of Chinese and Korean Major Container Terminals." *LISS 2012: Proceedings of Second International Conference on Logistics, Informatics and Service Science*, edited by Z. Zhang, R. Zhang, and J. Zhang, 163–68. New York: Springer.

Martín Bofarull, M. 2003. "Avances de productividad en el sistema portuario español." Paper presented at the Sixth Meeting of Applied Economics, Granada, Spain, June 5, 6, and 7.

Martínez-Budría, E., R. Díaz-Armas, M. Navarro-Ibañez, and T. Ravelo-Mesa. 1999. "A Study of the Efficiency of Spanish Port Authorities Using Data Envelopment Analysis." *International Journal of Transport Economics* 26 (2): 237–53.

Mokhtar, K. 2013. "Technical Efficiency of Container Terminal Operations: A DEA Approach." *Journal of Transportation Systems Engineering and Information Technology* 6 (2): 1–19.

Mokhtar, K., and M. Z. Shah. 2013. "Malmquist Productivity Index for Container Terminal." *European Journal of Business and Management* 5 (2): 91–106.

Park, R.-K., and P. De. 2004. "An Alternative Approach to Efficiency Measurement of Seaports." *Maritime Economics and Logistics* 6 (1): 53–69.

Rios, L. R., and A. C. Gastaud Maçada. 2006. "Analysing the Relative Efficiency of Container Terminals of Mercosur Using DEA." *Maritime Economics and Logistics* 8 (4): 331–46.

Schoyen, H., and J. Odeck. 2013. "The Technical Efficiency of Norwegian Container Ports: A Comparison to Some Nordic and UK Container Ports Using Data Envelopment Analysis (DEA)." *Maritime Economics and Logistics* 15 (2): 197–221.

Song, B., and Y. Cui. 2014. "Productivity Changes in Chinese Container Terminals 2006–2011." *Transport Policy* 26: 377–384.

Suárez-Alemán, A., L. Trujillo, and K. B. P. Cullinane. 2014. "Time at Ports in Short Sea Shipping: When Timing Is Crucial." *Maritime Economics and Logistics* 16: 399–417.

Tongzon, J. 2001. "Efficiency Measurement of Selected Australian and Other International Ports Using Data Envelopment Analysis." *Transportation Research Part A* 35 (2): 107–22.

Turner, H., R. Windle, and M. Dresner. 2004. "North American Container Port Productivity: 1984/1997." *Transportation Research Part E* 40 (4): 339–56.

Valentine, V. F., and R. Gray. 2001. "The Measurement of Port Efficiency Using Data Envelopment Analysis." *Proceedings of the Ninth World Conference on Transport Research*, Seoul, July 22–27.

Wang, T. and K. P. B. Cullinane. 2006. "The Efficiency of European Container Terminals and Implications for Supply Chain Management." *Maritime Economics & Logistics* 8 (1): 82–99.

Wilmsmeier, G., B. Tovar, and R. Sanchez. 2013. "The Evolution of Container Terminal Port Productivity and Efficiency under Changing Economic Environments." *Research on Transport Business and Management* 8: 50–66.

# Competition Index

Table B.1 **Competition Indexes of Selected Ports**

| Port | Component score | | | | | |
| | Country market share | Geographic concentration | Containerization | Transshipment | Intraport market structure | Index[a] |
|---|---|---|---|---|---|---|
| JNPT | 1 | 3 | 3 | 1 | 3 | 2.2 |
| Colombo | 1 | 1 | 3 | 3 | 2 | 2.0 |
| Mundra | 2 | 3 | 2 | 1 | 3 | 2.2 |
| Kandla | 3 | 3 | 1 | 2 | 1 | 2.0 |
| Karachi | 1 | 3 | 2 | 1 | 3 | 2.0 |
| Kolkata | 3 | 1 | 2 | 2 | 2 | 2.0 |
| Mumbai | 3 | 3 | 1 | 2 | 1 | 2.0 |
| Pipavav | 3 | 2 | 3 | 1 | 1 | 2.0 |
| Cochin | 3 | 2 | 1 | 2 | 1 | 1.8 |
| Tuticorin | 3 | 1 | 2 | 2 | 1 | 1.8 |
| Qasim | 1 | 3 | 2 | 1 | 1 | 1.6 |
| Chennai | 2 | 1 | 3 | 1 | 1 | 1.6 |
| Mongla | 3 | 1 | 2 | 1 | 1 | 1.6 |
| Mormugao | 3 | 2 | 1 | 1 | 1 | 1.6 |
| New Mangalore | 3 | 2 | 1 | 1 | 1 | 1.6 |
| Visakhapatnam | 3 | 1 | 1 | 2 | 1 | 1.6 |
| Chittagong | 1 | 1 | 1 | 1 | 1 | 1.0 |

*Note:*
a. Index is simple average of scores for five categories, which range from 1 (lowest) to 3 (highest), based on performance between 2000 and 2010.

# Data Sources

**Table C.1  Sources of Data Used in This Report**

| Chapter | Variable | Source of data | Period | Link (if available) |
|---|---|---|---|---|
| 1 | Port throughput (worldwide) | World Development Indicators | 2000–13 | http://data.worldbank.org /indicator/IS.SHP.GOOD .TU/countries |
| | Container port throughput in India | *Basic Port Statistics of India* | 2000–14 | http://shipping.nic.in/showfile. php?lid=1980 |
| | Container port throughput in Bangladesh | Chittagong and Mongla port authorities | 2000–13 | http://cpa.gov.bd/; http://mpa .gov.bd/ |
| | Container port throughput in Maldives | Maldives Port Authority | 2000–13 | http://www.port.com.mv/ |
| | Container port throughput in Pakistan | Karachi and Qasim port authorities | 2000–13 | http://kpt.gov.pk/; http://www .pqa.gov.pk/ |
| | Container port throughput in Sri Lanka | Colombo Port Authority | 2000–13 | http://www.slpa.lk/ |
| | Private sector investment commitments | PPIAF database | 1990–14 | http://ppi.worldbank.org/ |
| | Container port facilities added (2000–10) | *Containerisation International Yearbook* | 2000–10 | |
| | Indian port capacity and traffic | Ministry of Shipping of India | 1998–14 | http://shipping.nic.in/ |
| | Container-handling tariffs | Safmarine | 2014 | www.safmarine.com |
| | Time partial performance indicators | *Basic Port Statistics of India* and port authority websites | 2000–12 | http://shipping.nic.in/showfile .php?lid=1980 |
| | Average turnaround time by region | OECD | 1996–11 | http://www. internationaltransportforum .org/jtrc/DiscussionPapers /DP201408.pdf |
| 2 | South Asian port facilities and throughput | *Containerisation International Yearbook* | 2000–10 | |
| | Planned and actual investments at Indian ports | Ministry of Shipping of India | 2002–17 | http://shipping.nic.in/ |

*table continues next page*

**Table C.1  Sources of Data Used in This Report** *(continued)*

| Chapter | Variable | Source of data | Period | Link (if available) |
|---|---|---|---|---|
| | Private sector involvement at South Asian ports | Port authorities' and terminal operators' websites | 2015 | Various sources |
| | Private participation in South Asia | PPIAF database | 2000–10 | http://ppi.worldbank.org/ |
| | Board governance data | Port authorities' websites and professional online networks | 2014 | Various sources, including www .linkedin.com |
| 3 | Container port throughput in India | *Basic Port Statistics of India* | 2000–14 | http://shipping.nic.in/showfile .php?lid=1980 |
| | Container port throughput in Bangladesh | Chittagong and Mongla port authorities | 2000–13 | http://cpa.gov.bd/; http://mpa .gov.bd/ |
| | Container port throughput in Maldives | Maldives Port Authority | 2000–13 | http://www.port.com.mv/ |
| | Container port throughput in Pakistan | Karachi and Qasim port authorities | 2000–13 | http://kpt.gov.pk/; http://www .pqa.gov.pk/ |
| | Container port throughput in Sri Lanka | Colombo Port Authority | 2000–13 | http://www.slpa.lk/ |
| | Transshipment at Indian ports | *Basic Port Statistics of India* | 2003–12 | http://shipping.nic.in/showfile .php?lid=1980 |
| | Transshipment at Sri Lankan port | Colombo Port Authority | 2003–12 | http://www.slpa.lk/ |
| | Port facilities and operators by terminal | Port authorities' websites | 2014 | |
| 4 | Trade and economic growth statistics | World Bank database | 2000–13 | http://data.worldbank.org/topic /economy-and-growth |
| | Logistics performance indicators | LPI World Bank database | 2014 | http://lpi.worldbank.org/ |
| | Maritime transport costs | OECD Maritime Transport Cost dataset | 2000–07 | http://stats.oecd.org/Index .aspx?DataSetCode=MTC |
| | Exports to United States by country | UN Comtrade database | 2000–07 | http://comtrade.un.org/ |
| | Maritime distances | sea-distances.org | | sea-distances.org |
| | Connectivity | Liner Shipping Connectivity Index | 2000–07 | http://data.worldbank.org /indicator/IS.SHP.GCNW.XQ |

www.ingramcontent.com/pod-product-compliance
Lightning Source LLC
Chambersburg PA
CBHW080926050426
42334CB00055B/2793